THE TAMBRAM'S RECIPES

JAYSHREE M. SUNDAR

White Falcon
Publishing

www.whitefalconpublishing.com

The Tambram's Recipes
Book Concept and Author Jayshree M. Sundar
Recipes by Sundar Rajagopalan
Photography by Jayshree M. Sundar and Sundar Rajagopalan
Cover Art and Design by Kartika Bagodi
Illustrations and Art Direction by Kartika Bagodi (@crisprocks)
Project Management by Jayati Mukherjee
Creative inputs by Tarini Sundar

www.whitefalconpublishing.com

ISBN – 978-1-63640-351-9

THE
TAMBRAM'S
RECIPES

For Lady T

Your constant reaching out
for voice notes or making
phone calls for recipes
inspired this idea. A
ready reckoner for you
and your tribe!
Pour love and magic
into food like your papa.
And for our little love with
dotted paws – Roya.

WHY THIS BOOK?

For fun, I call my husband The Tambram.
The Tambram has some unique recipes. He is amazing as a cook. Influenced by both Tamil Nadu and Kerala in his growing years, the food he represents in this book has interesting nuances.

The Tambram is not a chef by training but by trial and innovation. For most of his life, he donned a management hat. He worked with India's largest news organization in various capacities from Publisher to Director, to internet company CEO. He started popular portals like magicbricks.com, and maybe, one of his most fun work opportunities was organizing the homecoming of the line-ups of Miss India's– star-studded Economic Times events, and so much more. A man of many talents, he is affectionately called the Don of our extended family. But through it all, his relaxation zone was the time spent in crafting a dish here, a meal there, and testing out new ideas and methods.

His mother taught him all the basics; his father later shared his special tricks. Yet the Tambram has his personal style and he does whip up the most delectable surprises!

The pandemic put a spotlight on his cooking. People called from far and wide, for his help. Prime among them was our daughter Tarini, who from this point forward will be referred to as Lady T. "Papa can you tell me how to make *upma*?" followed up with, "Papa it is getting lumpy – what do I do?" At other times, "How do I make my *dosa* crisp?" When Lady T made the dishes, her friends entered food paradise.

I always find the Tambram patiently writing recipes and sending tips to those who ask.

On a recent call with the extended family, he was urged to collate his recipes into a Word Document.

This got me thinking. Why a Word Document? Would that do justice to his talent?

Instead, I thought, we should create a useful tool. And in my mind, I positioned it as the simplest starter kit for food – a book that answers your cooking questions!

Within these pages are answers to the following:

How do you make the softest *idlis*?
What are all the ingredients you need in your kitchen to prepare a quick meal?
How can you make the creamiest *upma*?
What's the tactic to spread the roundest *dosa*?
How do you make really good curd rice?
How to cook with very little oil?
When to boil/steam/fry?
How do I cut veggies the right way?

N. Rajagopalan and Seetha Rajagopalan – both parents wonderful at cooking, whose influence has shaped the Tambram.

With today's emphasis on vegetarianism and health, this would be a perfect offering for those who want to learn how to cook but have no inclination to go for cooking classes, and are crushed for time. This book might work as an antidote to homesickness. But most importantly, it is for those who want a good meal!

These recipes come to you by a man who's lived an utterly busy life. He has put a bouquet of offerings to aid you. No recipe here will take ages or tire you out. Many simple options with one or two ingredients are there as well.

Health

Very little oil is used in South Indian cooking. Often only for tempering. This book has a number of one spoon-oil dishes.

Ghee or clarified butter is making such a comeback as a healthy option. It's integral to many recipes in his repertoire.

Vegetables have unique flavours and these recipes bring those out.

Fermentation is an often-used method. Very good for gut bacteria.

Steaming of the most popular foods – *idlis*, ripe bananas, etc.

A few tasty non-vegetarian items like eggs, chicken, and mutton are also included.
Look out for the #editorschoice

The Tambram's methods

The Tambram is a man of economy with words but cooking brings out a different side of him.
He customizes to suit people's tastes and palate while spending hours in the kitchen very happily, often with no one around. Usually on a quiet Saturday afternoon. The result could be a surprising chutney which you've never eaten elsewhere, a delicious *avial*, a sweet, or the tamarind rice from his repertoire.

I notice his behaviour in the kitchen. He likes to work alone. He never leaves a mess behind. While cooking, he gives each step time, and is a perfectionist, without being painful about it. When he tastes below par food made by others, he has an air of an expert about him. "Give me five minutes – I will repair it". He hates to complicate recipes. His list of ingredients is to the point and so are his steps.

So for those of you who lead busy lives but still want to be experts in the kitchen, I would like to extend an invitation to you. For the lovers of good food and health. For those culinary experts who haven't been exposed to recipes from Tamil Nadu and Kerala.

Here is your personal food guide, and crisis manager.

The Tambram's recipes.

Now let's get started.

contents

contents

Please refer to the Glossary for the English/Hindi/Tamil version of the ingredients used in the book.

FOOD IS ESSENTIAL TO LIFE. WHY NOT GET PASSIONATE ABOUT COOKING?

breakfast

THE SOFTEST IDLIS

Prep time: 20 mins
Cooking time: 20 mins
Serves: 6-8 people

Ingredients:

2 glasses *Idli Rice*
1 glass *Split Urad Dal*
1 tbsp Salt
Oil for greasing
Water as required
 Idli Rice is not the normal cooking rice found at home. It is not *Basmati* or *Ponni*. You can purchase *idli rice* at a South Indian store near your house. Or you can get it online. It is shorter, flatter and thicker. You can also purchase readymade batter.)

Method:

To prepare the batter:

○ Wash and soak two glasses of *idli rice* and one glass of *split urad dal* separately in plenty of water for four to five hours.

○ Grind the rice to a slightly coarse consistency in a mixer-grinder. The batter should be thick enough to fall off the spoon smoothly.

○ Grind the *urad dal* to a soft, smooth and fluffy batter in a mixer-grinder using little water. The batter should fall off the spoon smoothly.

○ Pour the rice batter first in a big container followed by the *dal* batter and add the salt.

○ Using a large spoon, mix the batter together in quick, circular movements for at least 3 to 4 minutes.

○ Cover it properly and let it ferment overnight or for 8 to 10 hours in summer and 12 to 14 hours in winter.

To cook the Idlis:

○ Grease the *idli* moulds (preferably with *til* oil) and pour one spoon of the batter in each disk. Keep about one inch of water in the *idli* maker or pressure cooker and let it come to a boil and start producing steam.

○ Place the *idli* stand with the batter into this hot steaming vessel. Cover the lid without the weight and let a strong gush of steam come out.

○ Steam for 15 minutes then turn off the flame.

○ Open the *idli* maker/pressure cooker after it cools down in 4 to 5 mins.

○ De-mould *idlis* with a blunt knife.

Tambram's Tip

1. *If you are in a hurry, pour water on the reverse side of the moulds to do a quick cool before de-moulding.*

2. *In winter, cover the entire vessel with a blanket or towel to aid the fermenting process and place it near the heater.*

3. *Add just enough water while grinding the batter, neither too much, nor too little. The finished batter should be soft and velvety. If the batter is watery or runny, the Idlis will be flat and hard – so add water very carefully while grinding to get the correct consistency and mix the dough well.*

4. *You will see small bubbles, get a sour smell in a well fermented batter.*

5. *After placing the idli stand in the cooker/idli maker, leave it open without closing the lid for a few minutes. In my experience this makes the idlis softer.*

6. *If you take the batter out of the fridge the next day, keep it out for an hour at room temperature, before making idlis.*

7. *To heat cold idlis, I sprinkle water and cover it with moist cloth and microwave it for 15/20 seconds and serve it hot.*

Variation:

You can put them in small moulds and serve as Cocktail *idlis*.

Serving Suggestion:

Serve hot with *sambhar* and Coconut Chutney.
Or with Gun powder (*Molagapodi)* and *til* oil.

Did you know?
Health details – The fermentation process increases the absorption of proteins and enhances the vitamin B content in this dish. Idlis are a great source of carbohydrates and protein.
Oil is required for greasing and not cooking and I prefer to use til oil for greasing the pan.
Zero oil dish.
Each idli is approx. 39 calories.

STeaMeD NeNDRaM PaZHaM

Prep time: 3 mins
Cooking time: 7 mins
Serves: 2-3 people

Steamed Kerala Banana

Ingredients:

2 or 3 Ripe Kerala Bananas
Water for steaming
Grated Jaggery to taste (optional)
Honey for drizzling (optional)

Did you know?
Health details – Ripe and steamed bananas are very easy to digest. Can be given to babies too. No white sugar yet a sweet dish. Good for breakfast or a snack. Ghee, jaggery, honey, or just the plain bananas are all power foods. High in potassium.

Method:

○ Cut the ends and chop each banana into an inch-thick pieces.
○ Fill 1 ½ inches of water in pressure cooker for steaming (you can also use your *idli* stand or any steamer).
○ Place the banana pieces on the stand, shut the lid and let it steam for 6 to 7 minutes.

Serving Suggestion:

Serve with honey (optional), peeled or unpeeled.

Variation:

Boil the bananas with a small serving of jaggery to add to the sweetness.

Tambram's Tip

Get bananas with almost black skin. Such bananas are properly ripe for steaming.

After the steaming, I sometimes take a pan and put in a spoon of ghee and coat the steamed bananas with it. I sauté for a few minutes for a crispy and delicious dessert.

You can sauté the bananas in ghee instead of steaming them.

UPMa

Prep time: 5 mins
Cooking time: 15 mins
Serves: 2 people

Ingredients:

2 to 3 cups of Semolina, lightly dry

1 medium sized Onion, chopped fine
1 medium sized Tomato, chopped fine
½ inch Ginger, skinned and chopped fine

Urad Dal
2 Green Chillies, split into halves
1 sprig of Curry Leaves (optional)
Ghee (optional)

Method:

○ Put water to boil in a pan.
○ Heat oil in another pan. Crackle mustard seeds and add *urad dal* and sauté until golden.
○ Add split chillies, tomato, onion, and ginger. Put curry leaves, if you want. Roast until the onion is translucent.
○ Add boiling water and salt.
○ Reduce the heat and start sprinkling semolina into the boiling water. Stir to ensure no lumps are formed. Keep stirring and check for salt.
○ Once the semolina absorbs all the water yet retains moisture, add *ghee*.

Tambram's Tip

When you sprinkle semolina in the boiling water, use a long-handled spoon to stir as the excess water starts popping and can scald your hand.

Serving Suggestion:

Serve hot with a cup of coffee.

CRISPY DOSA

Prep time: overnight
Cooking time: 5 mins per dosa
Serves: 6-8 people

The king of all savoury pancakes/crepes

Ingredients:

For the batter:

2 glasses *Dosa Rice*
1 glass *Split Urad Dal*
1 tbsp Salt
Water as required

For spreading:

Til oil/*Ghee*

Flat Spoon

Scoop Spoon

Method:

○ Wash and soak two glasses of *dosa rice* and one glass of *split urad dal* separately in plenty of water for four to five hours.

○ Grind the rice to a smooth consistency in a mixer-grinder. The batter should be thick but fall off the spoon smoothly.

○ Grind the *dal* to a soft, smooth, and fluffy batter in a mixer-grinder using little water. The batter should fall off the spoon smoothly.

○ Pour the rice batter first in a big container and follow with the *dal* batter. Add the salt. Then take a large spoon and mix the batter together thoroughly using quick and rapid circular movements for 3 to 4 minutes.

○ Cover it well and let it ferment overnight or for 8 to 10 hours in summer and 12 to 14 hours in winter. The batter will be thick, fluffy, and will rise after fermentation. Take out the required quantity to make a few *dosas* in a smaller mixing bowl and add a little water to get the right pouring and spreading consistency.

○ Take a non-stick *dosa* pan. Add a few drops of oil to the pan. Wipe off the excess with a kitchen towel or tissue paper. Traditionally, people cut an onion into half and use the flat-cut side to spread oil on the pan.

○ Turn the heat on high and let the pan warm up. Once it's hot turn the gas to medium. Now using a long handled flat bottomed scoop spoon, pour the batter onto the pan.

○ Quickly, with the flat back of the spoon, spread the dough out from the centre making concentric circles. Make sure the spoon remains by and large in the centre and keep spreading.

○ The *dosa* should cook on medium to low heat. Within minutes, you will see a number of bubbles forming and bursting into holes on the surface. Take a small teaspoon of oil and put a few drops around the *dosa*.

○ As it cooks, the edge of the *dosa* will lift off the pan. Once the sides lift up, take a flat wooden or metal spoon and run it around and under the *dosa*, loosening it so that it can be flipped.

○ Flip it and let it cook for a few seconds.

Tambram's Tip

Use til oil when frying the dosa for the correct taste.

My mother sometimes soaked fenugreek seeds along with the rice to make the dosa extra soft. This is optional. I only do this sometimes.

If the batter gets stuck on the pan, it means the pan is too hot. Lift the pan off the flame for a few minutes. Reduce heat.
If the dough is too runny, add batter.

Serving Suggestion:

Serve hot with chutney and *sambhar*.

Variation:

You can use *ghee* or clarified butter to crisp the sides when cooking the *dosa*.

For crispy *dosas*, spread the batter thinner; so take a little less on your ladle. Spread oil or *ghee* generously all over the *dosa* and not just the sides. Wait for the *dosa* to become brownish in colour before flipping it.

For soft *dosas* make smaller sized ones and spread the dough thick.

Dosa with Til oil and Molgapodi

ven pongal

Prep time: 5 mins
Cooking time: 7 mins
Serves: 3-4 people

Rice and lentil dish

Ingredients:

1 cup of Rice
1 cup of *Yellow Moong Dal*
1 tsp of Salt (add to taste)
3 tsp of *Ghee*
1 tsp of Black Peppercorn
1 tsp Cumin Seeds
A small piece of Ginger, thinly sliced
Pinch of *Hing*
8 Curry Leaves

Method:

○ Dry roast the *moong dal* taking care it does not darken.

○ Once done, add the *dal* and rice in the cooker for 5 mins. Once it is soft and mushy, add salt and mix well.

○ Temper it with lightly crushed black peppercorn, cumin, ginger, and *hing*.

○ Then add curry leaves.

Serving Suggestion:

Serve with coconut chutney.

Variation:

Sweet Pongal/Shakara Pongal
Use the same process of cooking the rice and *dal* in the same proportion without peppercorn, salt, cumin, and ginger. Add 3 pods of cardamom seeds and stir in.
Once the rice and *dal* is cooked, add a cup of jaggery and mix well. The rice will become dark brown.
For decoration and presentation add 6/8 cashew nuts fried in a little *ghee* and put it on top of the finished *Pongal*.
Made during *Sankranti* festival, it can be a dessert all year long!

Tambram's Tip

I add peppercorn (without crushing) and allow it to boil with rice and dal. I add ghee a bit more generously.

vermicelli upma

Prep time: 5 mins
Cooking time: 20 mins
Serves: 3 people

Semiya Upma

Ingredients:

2 tbsp Oil
1 tsp Mustard Seeds
4 tbsp Peanuts
1 tsp *Urad Dal*
1 tbsp *Chana Dal*
7–8 Curry leaves
1 Onion, sliced into long pieces
1 tsp Ginger, chopped fine
2 Green Chillies
1 tsp Salt
1 ½ cup Vermicelli
1 ¼ cup Water

Method:

○ In a pan, dry roast the vermicelli till it turns reddish brown. Set aside on a plate.

○ In the same pan, add the oil, add mustard seeds. When it crackles, add the *urad chana dal,* and peanuts, then roast till the *dals* turns golden brown.

○ Add curry leaves and chopped green chillies. Give it a stir.

○ Add the onion and ginger and stir till the onion turns translucent.

○ Now add the water (preferably warm or hot). Then add salt, and the vermicelli. Keep it covered for 3–4 mins, on medium heat.

○ Open the lid and check if the vermicelli is cooked by tasting a bit. If it needs further cooking, remove the lid and give it a gentle stir till it cooks.

Serving Suggestion:

Best served as soon as it's cooked.

Tambram's Tip

I use store-bought roasted peanuts. In case you have raw peanuts, deep fry them.
If the vermicelli gets dry and sticky, sprinkle water and stir.

Variation:

You can add 3 tbsp of finely chopped beans, carrots, and peas. Add them in after frying the onions. Put about 2 tbsp water and cover and cook for 3–4 mins or until vegetables are cooked. This makes the dish more filling and a complete meal.

Did you know?
Health details – Being high in energy and carbohydrates, it is a nutritious diet for both children and adults, especially when the vegetables are added.

THROW THE BEST BRUNCH PARTY

Have you ever wondered what medley of dishes to serve for a brunch you may be organising? Generally it is a mix of Western and Indian cuisine or North (typically Punjabi) and South Indian mashup.

Well here's an idea – make it completely South Indian!

Research proves that the most popular food in India is the *Idli*. In western countries, people go out "for a *dosa*"! So how about calling in your friends or relatives for brunch with dishes that typify a culture?

Start with a welcome drink. A piping hot glass of *Rasam*. Accompany it with small pieces of roasted *Pappadum*.

The next course could be Cocktail *Idlis*, Tomato *Upma*, string hoppers, and hot-hot *Dosas*. Of course with *Sambhar* and chutney. You could add *Shundal* and *Paniyaram* to make it distinctive.

For the non-vegetarians, serve Pepper Chicken Drumsticks.

Round off all this with a delicious shot of filter coffee. The South Indian variety.

A wonderful way to create the cultural ambience is to use banana leaves as place mats and whorls of a few typical coloured flowers spread at the centre of the table. If you have steel utensils, you could serve the dishes in that.

I believe South Indian cuisine is absolutely the best food on offer for a mouth-watering, finger licking experience!

Hot Tomato Rasam

Served in Glasses

Karavadams

Mini Cocktail Idlis

Regular mini Idlis

Idlis coated with Molagapodi

Pan Fried mini Idlis

Crispy Dosa with Molgapodi and Til Oil

Medu Vada with Coconut Chutney and Sambhar

NOTHING
BRINGS
PEOPLE
TOGETHER
LIKE FOOD!

Meals

THE FINE ART OF CUTTING VEGETABLES

Boti

As a young girl, I spent a lot of summer vacations in Allahabad, my mother's ancestral home. Once the lunch menu was decided, my aunts and ma would sit on the floor with the traditional "Boti" (Indian knife) and cut vast quantities of vegetables with such expertise that it was like watching a fluid music and dance performance. The part which fascinated me the most was all of them shared the same veggies and cut them in the same way!

Years later when I got married, I was reacquainted with the fine art of cutting vegetables while watching my father-in-law. He was an excellent cook, but more than that his dishes had such uniformity of taste and were a visual delight due to the beauty and symmetry of the cut vegetables. He was efficient and put a lot of happy effort into the process.
My mother-in-law would tell me that no conversation on the menu needed to happen! Just by seeing the cut vegetables, she would know if a *sambhar*, *Kootu*, curry, *Avial*, or any of the other options should be cooked.

So dear reader, take note. Cut the vegetables according to the recipe you are planning to prepare. And while on this topic let's learn a little more.

Slice, mince, dice, cube, roundel, julienne—determine the visual appeal and the mouthfeel of the dish. That's the art. There is the science too. The way in which you cut fresh spices like garlic, ginger, or onions impacts the flavour profile you will create. The chemical composition of a vegetable when cut determines the overall taste and aroma of a dish. In the case of onions and garlic, a mince or a fine chop allows them to release enzymes that create sharper pungency and smell.
Always wash your vegetables before peeling them; not just to remove the dirt over them, but also to retain the water-soluble vitamins in the vegetables that you may lose if you wash them after peeling.

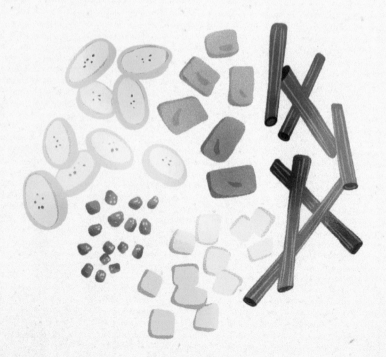

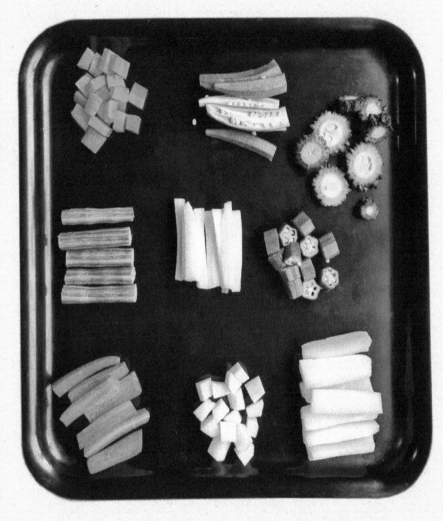

○ An *Avial* dish has the vegetables cut into long French fry-like shapes. With the same height and width. For *Avial*, you can use many varieties of vegetables – the Tambram usually puts in potatoes, sweet potatoes, carrots, beans, white pumpkin, raw banana, and drumsticks.

○ In the kitchen, the preferred cut determines the cooking time. For example, a relatively dry vegetable like beans would overcook very fast if you cut it too thin.

○ For *Olan*, cut the vegetables into big thin dices. You can prepare it using only ash gourd, but a mix of ash gourd and red pumpkin makes it interesting. Slice green chillies vertically into two and cook along with the vegetables.

○ For *Sambhar*, the vegetables are cut into big cubes and long for drumsticks and onion (small onions are put as a whole).

○ When potatoes for a simple roast are cut into small dices, the surface area is more. This makes them get crisp outside and soft inside. Small baby potatoes are used whole.

○ Tomatoes should be cut for gravy dishes with texture or where you need it to show it like *Rasam* and *Upma* and pureed for smooth gravy dishes.

○ Onions, when cubed or sliced in a semi-circle give a mild flavour. When pureed, onions will give a strong flavour.

○ Some vegetables have an edible skin with loads of vitamins and minerals. Know these veggies and try to keep their peel to get the most out of them. Some of these veggies are cucumbers, brinjals, and potatoes. Or with *Vazhai Tholl Thoran*, which is made from raw banana peel.

Grandmothers say that the more finely the vegetable is chopped, the faster they get spoilt. They lose moisture, natural colour, and some amount of nutrients. If you are planning to cut your vegetables and store them to be cooked later, try to cut them into bigger pieces. Shredded vegetables must be immediately cooked and consumed.

Keep in mind to cut or peel as close to the skin of the vegetables as possible. This way you'll get the maximum amount of nutrients from them.

coconut rice

Prep time: 5 mins
Cooking time: 15 mins
Serves: 2 people

Ingredients:

1 cup of Long Grain Rice
1 cup of Fresh Coconut, freshly grated (defrost well, if it is frozen)
1/2 tsp of Salt (add to taste)
Pinch of *Hing*
1/2 tsp of Ginger, finely chopped
1/2 tsp of Mustard Seeds

1 tsp of *Urad Dal*
2 tsp of *Chana Dal*
1 or 2 Dried Red Chillies (or according to taste)
10 Curry Leaves
3 to 4 tsp of Cooking Oil
3 to 4 tsp Cashew Nuts (optional)

Method:

○ Boil rice in enough water to ensure that the cooked rice grains are separate and not mushy.
○ Spread the cooked rice on a plate and separate the grains with a fork or spoon and let it cool down a bit.
○ In a pan add the cooking oil and sauté the cashew nuts. Remove once done.
○ Add mustard seeds in the oil. Let it crackle. Then add *urad dal* and *chana dal* and sauté till golden brown.
○ Then add *hing*, curry leaves, chopped ginger and broken red chillies. Stir for less than a minute and add the cashew nuts.
○ Switch off or minimize flame to very low.
○ Add the coconut, rice and salt and mix it well without mashing the rice.

Serving Suggestion:

Serve hot with pickle.

Tambram's Tip

A good dish to be made with leftover rice. You can also make it with fresh rice.

Did you know?
Health details – Coconut is high in fibre and rice has complex carbohydrates and is low in fibre. Rice provides the energy and fresh coconut aids in lowering cholesterol and weight loss.

TAKKALI RICE

Prep time: 7 mins
Cooking time: 20 mins
Serves: 2 people

Spicy Tomato Rice

Ingredients:

3 tsp Oil
1 tsp Mustard Seeds
½ tsp *Urad Dal*
½ tsp *Chana Dal*
¼ tsp Fenugreek Seeds
4 Cloves
Few Curry Leaves
Few Peanuts/Cashew Nuts
1 Onion, chopped fine
1 Green Chilli, slit

¼ tsp Ginger Paste
2 Garlic Pods
2 Tomatoes, chopped fine
¼ tsp Turmeric Powder
½ tsp Red Chilli Powder
½ tsp Salt
2 cups Rice, cooked
2 tbsp Coriander, chopped fine
1 tsp *Ghee*

Method:

○ In a large pan, heat 3 tsp oil and tip in the mustard seeds. Let it crackle
Add the methi seeds, *urad dal* and *chana dal*. Stir continuously until the
dals brown.

○ Sauté peanuts until golden brown.

○ Add onion, green chilli, ginger paste and sauté well; then add the curry leaves.
Now add tomatoes and sauté until tomatoes turn soft and mushy.

○ Add turmeric, chilli powder, coriander powder, and salt and sauté for a
minute; then put in the cooked rice and mix gently.

○ Cover and simmer for 5 minutes so that all the flavours mingle.

○ Slice a few tomatoes long and decorate on top. Add the coriander leaves.
Add a teaspoon of *ghee*.

Serving Suggestion:

Serve with thick yogurt or a *pachadi* and *appalam* .

Variation:

You can add cinnamon, cardamom, and cloves to the pan after
the *dals* are golden, if you want more spices.

Did you know?
Health details – this is a one dish meal – with the
goodness of rice, tomatoes and a lot of spices.
Very little oil.

Tambram's Tip

Add a half a teaspoon of
sambhar powder when you
add the rice. Mix well and let
it cook.
Can be made with leftover
rice. Just soak the old rice in
hot water for a couple of
minutes before using.

PULLYODHARAI

Prep time: 7 mins
Cooking time: 15 mins
Serves: 2 people

Tamarind Rice

Ingredients:

1 cup Rice
3 tbsp Oil
1 tsp Mustard seeds
1 tbsp *Chana Dal*
1 tsp *Urad Dal*
3 tbsp Raw Groundnut
8 to 10 Curry leaves
1 small lemon sized ball of Tamarind
3 tsp Sambhar powder
1 – 2 pinch *Hing*
1 – 2 whole Dried Red Chilies
Few Green Chillies (optional)
Salt to taste

Method:

Boil rice in enough water to ensure that the cooked rice grains are separate and not mushy.

Soak the tamarind in hot water and squeeze the extract 2 to 3 times adding more water. Throw away the remnant fibre. The tamarind extract should be about a cup.

Heat the oil in a pan and add mustard seeds. Once it splutters, add *urad dal*, *chana dal,* peanuts, and pieces of dried red chilli, and roast till the *dals* are brown.

Add curry leaves, and *hing* and stir for 2 minutes.

Add the tamarind extract and salt and let it boil and thicken until the raw smell of tamarind goes away.

Add rice along with oil or *ghee* and mix well.

Serving Suggestion:

Serve it hot with *appalams* or potato chips or *karuvadams.*

Tambram's Tip

*A quick dish with leftover rice.
I use sesame or til oil generously.*

*Did you know?
Health details – This dish has a long
shelf life due to the tamarind.
It's a great travel food and is rich in
fibre and protein.*

Tambram Aloo Rice

Prep time: 20 mins
Cooking time: 15 mins
Serves: 4 people

Ingredients:

3 large Potatoes
3 Green Chillies (optional)
1 tsp *Split Urad Dal*
½ tsp *Chana Dal*
2 pinches of *Hing*
Salt to taste
1 tsp of Turmeric Powder
1 tsp Chili Powder
4 to 5 tsp of Cooking Oil
8 or 10 Curry Leaves (optional)
1 tbsp *Ghee*
3 cups of cooked Rice

Method:

○ Boil the potatoes. Cut them into cubes. Set aside.
○ Heat oil in a pan. Add mustard seeds and let them splutter then quickly add *urad dal*, *chana dal* and *hing*. Add curry leaves (optional).
○ Once the *dals* are roasted to a golden brown, add the cubed potatoes.
○ Put the turmeric powder and chili powder and add salt to taste.
○ Add tiny pieces of green chilli if you want a really spicy flavour. Cook with the lid closed for 10 mins.
○ Open the lid and let it fry a bit more till the potatoes turn a golden brown.
○ Add cooked rice and fold in the potatoes gently together. Too much stirring can make this dish mushy.

Serving Suggestion:

Best served with *papadam* and tomato *pachadi* and *avakkai* (mango) pickle. Add a spoon or two of *ghee* just before serving.

Variation:

You can use 2 or 3 finely chopped lemon pickle pieces in the rice.

Did you know?
Health details – this is a meal in itself. It's very comforting and meets your carbohydrate requirements for the day.

Curd Rice

Prep time: 5 mins
Cooking time: 15 mins
Serves: 2–3 people

Ingredients:

1 cup of Rice – *Ponni*, if possible, or any other
2 to 3 cups of Curd
1 Green Chilli
1 tsp Salt

For the tempering:
1 tsp Cooking Oil
1 tsp Mustard Seeds
1 tsp *Urad Dal*
A pinch of *Hing*
6 Curry Leaves

Method:

○ Cook the rice till it is soft.
○ Mash the rice well while it is still hot. Then allow it to cool and add salt and curd and mix/mash it well.

For the tempering:
○ In a small pan heat oil. Put mustard seeds, *urad dal*, and *hing*. Let the mustard seeds splutter. Add curry leaves. Then pour the tempering over the curd rice.

Serving Suggestion:

Serve with *avakkai* or lemon pickle. *Mor Millagai* is also a traditional accompaniment with this dish.

Variation:

You can add a small portion of ginger, cut into tiny pieces. Or you can add a small portion of cucumber and raw mango cut into small thin pieces.
Some people add a few pomegranate seeds for colour and coriander leaves on the top for garnish and presentation.

Tambram's Tip

*If the rice is from the fridge and cold, heat it in the microwave and mash it.
I give it a quick spin in the mixer so that the rice grains break but the rice is not fully mashed-up. Be careful that you don't overgrind it.*

*Did you know?
Health details – Curd rice is typically the last course of every meal. The probiotic in the curd helps gut health. It's very soothing and delicious at the same time.*

Lemon Rice

Prep time: 5 mins
Cooking time: 10 mins
Serves: 2 people

Ingredients:

1 cup of Long-Grain Rice
Half Lemon (add more to taste)
½ tsp of Salt (add more to taste)
Pinch of *Hing*
½ tsp of *Haldi*
½ tsp of Mustard Seeds
1 tsp of *Urad Dal*
2 tsp of *Chana Dal*
One to two Green Chillies or Red Chillies or
both according to taste
10 Curry Leaves
3 to 4 teaspoons of Cooking Oil
3 to 4 tsps Peanuts or Cashew Nuts (optional)

Method:

○ Boil rice in enough water to ensure that the cooked rice grains are separate and not mushy.
○ Spread the cooked rice on a plate and separate the grains with a fork or spoon and let it cool down a bit.
○ In a pan add the cooking oil then sauté the cashew nuts/peanuts and remove once done.
○ Add mustard seeds in the oil. Let it crackle, then add *urad dal* and *chana dal* and sauté till the *dals* are golden brown.
○ Add *hing*, curry leaves, chopped ginger and broken red chillies and stir for less than a minute. Add the sautéed cashew nuts/peanuts.
○ Switch off or minimize flame to very low and add the rice and salt and mix it well without mashing the rice.
○ Take it off the flame and squeeze the lemon. Check for salt and the sourness of the lemon. Add more if required.

Serving Suggestion:

Serve hot with *appalam* or lemon pickle or both.

Did you know?
Health details – This is low in calories, rich in carbohydrate, vitamin c and minerals.

Tambram's Tip

Freshen old rice with this quick recipe –especially if you have unannounced guests or want a change. If you don't have appalams handy this delectable dish tastes very good with potato or banana chips or fryums.

Paruppu Podi Saddam

Prep time: 5 mins
Cooking time: 15 mins
Serves: 2-3 people

Dry Lentil Powder and Rice

Ingredients:

1 cup *Tuar Dal*
1/4 cup *Chana Dal*, roasted
5 Dry Red Chillies
1 tsp Whole Black Peppercorns
1/5 tsp Cumin Seeds (Jeera)
10 Curry Leaves
1/4 tsp *Hing*
Salt to taste
1 cup Rice, cooked
2 spoons *Ghee*

Method:

○ Heat a pan.
○ Turn gas to medium heat and roast all the ingredients till they turn golden brown then turn off the gas and set the ingredients aside.
○ Once cool, put all the ingredients in a blender/grinder including the roasted *chana dal* and make it to a fine powder.
○ Store it in an airtight container.

Pickle
Ghee
Paruppu Podi
White Rice

Tambram's Tip

I recommend making the powder and storing it in the fridge. Use when required. Add a dash to salads also.

Did you know?
Health details – When eaten with rice, papad, pickle, and ghee, it's a complete meal – fats, protein, and carbohydrates.

Serving Suggestion:

Serve *Paruppu Podi* with hot white rice and *ghee* and *sutta appalam* (roasted papad). Mix the *Podi* and rice well with the *ghee*. The yummiest treat awaits.

You can also pair it with a simple potato preparation.

KEERAI KOOTU

Light Spinach Stew

Prep time: 5-7 mins
Cooking time: 10 mins
Serves: 4 people

Ingredients:

1/2 cup *Moong Dal*
2 to 3 cups Spinach, chopped
1 tbsp Cumin Seeds
2 Dried Red Chillies (add more to taste)

For the tempering:
1 tsp Cooking Oil
1 tsp Mustard Seeds
1 tsp *Urad Dal*
A pinch of *Hing*

Method:

○ Boil the *moong dal* in a pressure cooker with turmeric for 5 mins or till it becomes soft.
○ Grind coconut, cumin seeds, and red chillies into a paste.
○ In a large pan, put the *keerai*/spinach in 3 cups of water, turmeric, and salt.
○ Cover and cook for 5 to 6 mins.
○ Add the coconut paste to the pan and simmer for few minutes.
○ Add the *dal*. (If the *dal* is watery, remove excess water and retain in a cup for later use, if required)
○ Let it simmer for three to four minutes till it all blends well.

For the tempering:
○ In a small pan heat oil. Put mustard seeds, *urad dal*, and *hing*. Let the mustard seeds splutter. You can also add one red chilli (whole or broken), if you want it spicy. Then pour the tempering over the *Keerai Kootu*.

Serving Suggestion:

Best served with steaming white rice, pickles, and *appalams* (a type of fryum) to accompany.

Variation:

You can use *tuar dal*. (*Thuvaram Paruppu* in Tamil)
If you like, add 2 or 3 crushed garlic pods while tempering.

Tambram's Tip

Chop the keerai/spinach fine to help blend with dal and coconut.

Did you know?
Health details – Spinach is rich in antioxidants, Iron, and vitamins. Dal is rich in protein. Coconut is rich in minerals and is also an antioxidant. This dish has only one teaspoon of oil.

Avial

Prep time: 25 mins
Cooking time: 20 mins
Serves: 4 people

A Medley of Vegetables in a Coconut and Yogurt Gravy

Ingredients:

2 cups of Ash Gourd
2 Carrots
2 Drumsticks
2 Potatoes
1 Raw Banana
8 Beans (add other beans as well)
6 Flat Beans
6 String Beans
1 Coconut

1 tbsp of Cumin Seeds
1 tsp of Coconut/Cooking Oil (optional)
2 to 3 Green Chillies
2 tsp of Salt (add to taste)
1 tsp Turmeric Powder
1 cup of Yogurt
8 to 10 Curry Leaves

Method:

To cut vegetables:

Ash Gourd into cubes of an inch
Carrots into one inch thick strips
Drumsticks into one and half inch pieces
Potatoes peeled and cubed to an inch
Raw Banana peeled and cubed to half inch
Beans into one inch lengths
Flat Beans into less than one inch lengths
String Beans into one inch lengths
Coconut desiccated to one cup

To make the *Avial:*

○ Boil all the chopped vegetables in 4 cups of water with turmeric powder for 12 to 15 mins. Ensure that the vegetables don't overcook and become mushy. They should retain their shape. Once cooked, add salt and let it simmer for few minutes.

○ Grind the coconut along with cumin seeds and green chilli into a paste.

○ Add the ground coconut paste to the vegetables and let it boil for another 5 mins, letting the veggies absorb the coconut flavour. Stir carefully to ensure that the vegetables don't break.

○ Reduce the flame and add the whisked/whipped curd and let it simmer for 2 mins.

○ Garnish it with curry leaves as is or sautéed in oil.

Serving Suggestion:

Serve hot with steaming rice and *appalam* for accompaniment.

Variation:

You can make this dish without yogurt. Use half a cup of boiled *tuar dal* and mix it with the veggies. Follow the same process.

Did you know?
Health details – extremely healthy with a multitude of vegetables with zero or 1 teaspoon of oil.

Tambram's Tip

The quantity of water has to be right to boil vegetables. The dish is not watery but has enough gravy. Drain excess water before adding salt.
Can add vegetables like taro roots (arbi), sweet potato, pumpkin (makes it a bit sweet), yam, malabar cucumber, or other kinds of beans (all except cluster beans, which makes it bitter). Choose a combination that suits your palate best from the above mentioned vegetables.

Urulai Kazhangu Roast

Prep time: 15 mins
Cooking time: 20 mins
Serves: 4 people

Potato Roast

A great accompaniment to sambhar, rasam, or curd/lemon/tamarind rice.

Ingredients:

- 4 Medium Potatoes
- 4 tbsp Cooking Oil
- ¼ tsp Mustard Seeds
- Small piece of Solid *Hing*
- ¼ tsp *Hing* powder
- 3 Red Chillies
- ½ tsp *Urad Dal*
- ¼ tsp *Chana Dal*
- Salt to taste
- ¼ tsp Turmeric Powder
- ¼ tsp Chilli Powder
- 8 Curry Leaves

Method:

- ○ Boil potatoes, peel, and cut into cubes.
- ○ In a pan, add oil and the small piece of solid *hing*. When oil is hot, add mustard seeds and let them sputter.
- ○ Add *urad dal* and *chana dal* and keep stirring with the spoon till they brown. Take care to not let them burn.
- ○ Add curry leaves and the dried red chillies.
- ○ Add potato cubes and stir it all together.
- ○ Put in turmeric powder, salt, and chilli powder and cook with the lid closed for 5 mins.
- ○ Open lid and let it fry for a bit on a low flame till the potatoes are roasted and crisp.

Tambram's Tip

Keep the flame low during the roasting process. That way it won't burn and will slowly crisp outside and remain soft inside. This preparation tastes good without chillies too.

Variation:

This dish can be made using small whole potatoes as well.

Alternatively, you can add a cup or two of cooked rice and add a bit more salt and sauté it with the roasted potatoes. Don't stir it too much, instead just fold the rice in. Serve hot with *papadam*, pickle and tomato *pachadi*.

Olan

Prep time: 10 mins
Cooking time: 20 mins
Serves: 3–4 people

Kerala Stew at its Tastiest

Ingredients:

3 cups Ash Gourd, chopped
3 cups Red Pumpkin, chopped
2 Green Chillies
½ cup Black Eyed Peas (optional)
2 cups Coconut Milk
1 tsp Coconut Oil (optional)
1 tsp Salt (add to taste)

Method:

○ Soak black eyed peas for 4 hours. Boil and set aside.
○ Remove the outer skin and the inside seeds of pumpkin and ash gourd and cut them into 1 inch square, thin pieces.
○ Boil the ash gourd first as it takes longer to cook. After 6 to 7 minutes of boiling add split green chillies and pumpkin and allow it to cook in water till almost done.
○ Drain most of the water and add 1 cup of coconut milk and let it simmer for 3 mins.
○ Add black eyed peas and salt.
○ Switch off the gas and add remaining coconut milk and the coconut oil.

Serving Suggestion:

Serve with hot rice.

Tambram's Tip

*Since the vegetables are sliced thin, stir gently, to ensure that they don't get mashed up.
If you are reheating this dish, be careful not to overheat it as the coconut milk can turn oily.*

*Did you know?
Health details – The dish is mainly boiled veggies and zero oil, if you choose not to put the coconut oil. Though one teaspoon of oil is a taste enhancer.*

sambHar

Prep time: 10 mins
Cooking time: 25 mins
Serves: 6 people

Ingredients:

A lemon sized Tamarind (approx. 32 grams or 1 &1/2 tbsp)
1 cup hot Water
½ tsp Turmeric Powder
2 tsp *Sambhar Podi*
½ tsp Mustard Seeds
Few Curry Leaves
1 Large Radish, cut into 3mm roundels
Salt to taste
1 cup + 1 fistful of *Tuar Dal*
A pinch of *Hing*
1 tsp Oil

Method:

○ Soak the tamarind in hot water and squeeze the extract 2 to 3 times adding more water. Throw the remnant fibre. Tamarind extract should be about 2/3 of a cup.

○ Add Turmeric, *sambhar podi*, and *hing*.

○ Heat oil in a pan, add mustard seeds and curry leaves. Once the mustard seeds splutter, add the tamarind extract.

○ Add the radish in the simmering tamarind extract.

○ Add salt to taste and let it cook until the raw tamarind smell goes and the radish turns a little translucent.

○ In another pan boil *tuar dal* until mushy. Then add the cooked *dal* to the radish tamarind mixture and bring it to boil.

Serving Suggestion:

Serve with hot rice and *appalam* or potato chips.

Variation:

You can sauté the radish slices to retain their shape. You can add finely chopped onions and garlic while sautéing before adding radish and tamarind water.

Tambram's Tip

Drain and retain excess water from boiled Dal before mushing. If the dish seems very thick, you can add this water to bring it to the required consistency.

KOSMALLI

Prep time: 10 mins
Cooking time: 5 mins
Serves: Multiple

Cucumber Side Dish

Ingredients:

1 cup *Green Gram Dal*
1 or 2 Cucumber
1 tsp Lemon juice/ grated raw mango

For the tempering:
1 tsp Cooking Oil
½ tsp Mustard Seeds
½ tsp *Urad Dal*
Pinch of *Hing*
1 Dried Red Chilli, finely chopped

Method:

○ Soak the *dal* in water for 45 minutes.
○ Peel cucumber and cut into small pieces or grate.
○ Drain water from *dal* and add cucumber then add salt to taste.
○ Put lemon juice or grated raw mango.

For the tempering:
○ To temper, heat the oil in a pan and add mustard seeds. Once they splutter, add *urad dal* and red chilli. Pour over cucumber and *dal* mixture and serve.

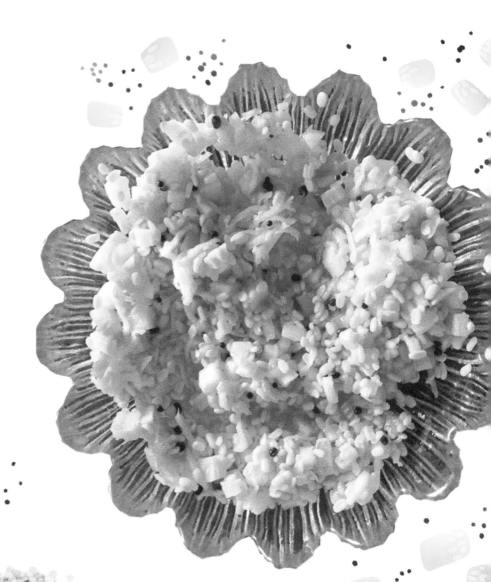

Serving Suggestion:

Best served with steaming white rice, pickles, and *appalams*.

BEETROOT PACHADI

Prep time: 7 mins
Cooking time: 10 mins
Serves: 1 as a salad meal, and 3 as side dish.

Ingredients:

2 cups Beetroot, grated
¾ cup Water
1 tsp Salt
Small cup Coconut, grated (optional)
1 Green Chilli
1 cup Curd/Yogurt, whisked

For the tempering:
½ tbsp Coconut Oil
1 tsp Mustard Seeds
2 Dried Red Chilli
Few Curry Leaves

Method:

○ In a large pan take 2 cups grated beetroot and ½ cup water (use the thicker side of the grater so that you get larger, grated pieces). Then add salt and mix well.

○ Cover and boil for 10 minutes. Switch off the gas and let it cool. Put it in the fridge once it has cooled.

○ In a nice salad bowl, take the yogurt and whisk it till it forms a thick paste. Add two tablespoons of water to make a good and smooth consistency.

○ Add the cooled, grated beetroot just before serving. Don't mix too much.

○ If you prefer the dish to have a red colour go ahead and mix it well.

For the tempering:

○ In a small pan, heat coconut oil. Add mustard seeds, dried red chilli, and curry leaves. Let the mustard seeds splutter. Pour the tempering over the *pachadi* and mix well.

○ Enjoy *beetroot pachadi* as a side dish to a meal.

Variation:

Take 1/2 a cup of fresh coconut, 1/2 tsp of cumin seeds, and a small piece of ginger and grind it with a little water.
Add it to the boiled beetroot and mix well.
Add more than one chili if you prefer it spicy.
In case you don't have coconut oil use your regular oil for tempering.

Did you know?
Health details – Beetroot is high in iron and yogurt is full of probiotics, and there's just one teaspoon of oil in this dish.

BHINDI PACHADI

Prep time: 5 mins
Cooking time: 10 mins
Serves: 4 people

Okra/Lady Finger Side Dish

Ingredients:

250 gms *Bhindi* (Okra/Lady Fingers)
2 tbsp Oil
Salt to taste
2 cups Yogurt
Pinch of Red Chilli Powder
Pinch of *Hing*

For the tempering:
2 Dried Red Chillies
1 tbsp Coconut Oil
1 tsp Mustard Seeds
10–12 Curry Leaves

Method:

○ Cut the okra into small roundels and add salt.
○ Heat oil in a pan and fry okra till they are crisp and brown.
○ Take off heat and set aside.
○ Put the curd in a serving bowl and add a spoon of water. Then whisk the curd to a smooth consistency. Don't make it watery. Add salt to taste, chilli powder, and *hing* and refrigerate.
○ Just before serving, put a layer of curd and top it with a layer of fried okra. Repeat. Don't mix. Make sure a thick layer of okra is on top.

For the tempering:
○ In a small pan, heat coconut oil. Add mustard seeds, cut, dried red chilli, and curry leaves. Let the mustard seeds splutter. Pour the tempering over the pachadi. Place it on the table and give it a very gentle swirl.

Tambram's Tip

When buying, choose okra that is free of bruises, is tender but not soft, and is about four inches long.
Add salt only after cutting the okra and patting it dry.
You can sprinkle rava (semolina) powder to the raw okra. Mix it well with your fingers. Then fry, it will add to the crispness.

Serving Suggestion:

Serve with a meal as a side dish or have it as a salad with *papadam*.

Variation:

Grind together: 2 tbsp freshly scraped coconut, 1 finely chopped green chilli, and 1 tsp finely chopped ginger. Add some water to make a smooth paste and add to the yogurt mixture.

You can add partly crushed peanuts for crunch.

Did you know?
Health details – A one dish salad bowl or a snack, Okra is easy to digest. Yogurt is a good probiotic and is rich in protein.

TOMATO PACHADI

Prep time: 5 mins
Cooking time: 10 mins
Serves: 2–3 people

Ingredients:

4 Tomatoes
500 gms Yogurt
2 Green Chillies
Salt to taste
¼ tsp Red Chili Powder

For the tempering:
½ tsp Mustard Seeds
Pinch of *Hing*
1 tsp Oil

Method:

○ Dice tomato into small pieces then remove excess water from the seeds.
○ In a large salad bowl tip in the entire quantity of yogurt. Add just a spoon or two of water and beat it to a thick consistency.
○ Add salt to taste.
○ Add the chilli powder, green chillies, and the tomato pieces and mix well.

For the tempering:
○ In a small pan, heat oil. Add mustard seeds and let them splutter. Add a pinch of *hing* and pour the tempering over the *pachadi* and mix.

Variation:

You can add a finely cut onion to this salad.

Did you know?
Health details – it's full of probiotics and good for gut health. It uses only one teaspoon of oil.

Tambram's Tip

This dish can be had as a mini meal/snack in itself with a few chips or fryums. Make the yogurt mixture then refrigerate. Cut the tomatoes and keep them ready in a box. Just assemble and temper before serving to keep all ingredients crisp.

vazhaikkai mezhukku varati

Prep time: 5–7 mins
Cooking time: 10 mins
Serves: 3–4 people

Raw Banana Coated with Oil

Ingredients:

2 Raw Banana
10 to 15 Yard Long Beans
2 Green Chillies
1 tsp Turmeric Powder
1 tsp Salt (add to taste)
2 to 3 tbsp of Cooking Oil

Did you know?
Health details – Raw banana is rich in vitamins and minerals iron high fibre, low on glycaemic index. String beans are rich in vitamins, folic acid and fibre.

Method:

○ Scrape the banana (retaining the peel adds to the nutrition value) and cut into small half an inch cubes. Then soak in turmeric water to retain its colour.
○ Cut Beans into one inch length pieces.
○ Boil both the veg in turmeric water for 10 mins. Add salt when it is almost cooked. Once done, drain the water and set aside.
○ Heat oil in a pan. Gently crush the green chillies and put into the oil. Immediately thereafter add the boiled veg and sauté it for 5 mins.

Serving Suggestion:

Good accompaniment to *mor khuzhambu*, *sambhar*, and *rasam*.

TOMATO RASAM

Spicy Tomato Soup

Prep time: 10 mins
Cooking time: 5 mins
Serves: Multiple

Serving Suggestion:

Serve it with hot rice and *aloo* roast or *appalams* or *karuvadams*.

Ingredients:

½ cup *Tuar Dal*
A lemon sized Tamarind (approx 32 grams or 1 &1/2 tbsp)
1 Tomato
1 – 1 ½ tsp Rasam Powder
1 – 2 pinches of *Hing*
1 – 1 ½ tsp Salt (add to taste)
Few sprigs of Coriander Leaves

For the tempering:
½ tsp Mustard Seeds
1 – 2 tsp *Ghee*

Method:

○ Soak the tamarind in hot water and squeeze the extract 2 to 3 times adding more water. Throw the remnant fibre. Tamarind extract should be about 2 cups or more.

○ Alongside, cook the *dal* well till it is mushy and soft in two cups of water. After cooking, if there is excess water, drain it and set it aside.

○ In the tamarind extract, add chopped tomato, *hing*, *rasam* powder, salt, turmeric powder and boil it for 7 to 8 minutes.

○ Mash the *dal* well and add it to the tamarind mixture, then let it simmer. When it starts foaming, turn off the stove. *Rasam* is usually watery, unlike *sambhar*, hence add water, if necessary.

For the tempering:
○ Temper with mustard seeds crackled in hot *ghee* then garnish with coriander leaves as is or chopped.

Variation:

The same recipe can be made with lemon or pepper alternatively.
You can use curry leaves also.
Add a green chilli if you want it spicy–(*Rasam* powder usually has spice).

Lemon Rasam

Prep time: 10 mins
Cooking time: 25 mins
Serves: 6 people

Ingredients:

1/2 cup *Tuar Dal*
Half Lemon (add more to taste)
1 Tomato
Small portion of crushed Ginger
½ tsp Red Chilli Powder
Less than ⅓ tsp of Turmeric Powder
1 Green Chilli
1 –2 pinches of *Hing*
1 tsp Salt (add to taste)
A small portion of fresh Coriander Leaves
1 tbsp *Ghee*

For the tempering:

½ tsp Mustard Seeds
1 - 2 tsp *Ghee*

Method:

○ Cook the *dal* in 2 cups of water until it is mushy and soft.
○ Put the chopped tomato, hing, crushed ginger, diced green chili, salt, turmeric powder and a large cup of water in a pan. Let it boil till tomatoes get soft and mushy. It should take about 5 mins.
○ Mash the *dal* well.
○ Mix the two and let it simmer. When it starts foaming, turn off the stove and add the lemon juice.

For the tempering:

○ Temper with mustard seeds crackled in hot *ghee* then garnish with coriander leaves as is or chopped.

Serving Suggestion:

Serve hot with rice, *aloo* roast and *appalam* or *karuvadams*.

Pepper-Cumin Rasam

Prep time: 10 mins
Cooking time: 25 mins
Serves: 6 people

Ingredients:

1 small lemon-sized ball of Tamarind
1 tsp Crushed Pepper/Pepper Powder
1 ½ tsp Cumin Powder
2 pinches Turmeric Powder
½ tsp Salt (add more to taste)
7/8 Curry Leaves

For the tempering:

½ tsp Mustard seeds
1 - 2 tsp *Ghee*

Method:

○ Soak the tamarind in 1 cup of hot water and take out the extract.
○ Put it in a pan with 1 more cup of water.
○ Then add turmeric powder, pepper powder, *jeera* powder and salt along with the curry leaves and let it boil for 6 to 8 mins, till the raw smell of tamarind disappears. Add more water. Let it simmer till it starts foaming.

For the tempering:

○ Temper with mustard seeds in hot *ghee* then garnish with coriander leaves.

Serving Suggestion:

Serve with hot rice and roasted *papadam*.

Tambram's Tip

Very good for a sniffling cold and cough– it opens up the nasal passages and gives quick relief.

KOTHAVARANGI PARUPPU USLI

Prep time: 10 mins
Cooking time: 5 mins
Serves: Multiple

Cluster Beans-Tambram Style!

Ingredients:

250 gms Cluster Beans
¾th cup *Toor Dal*
1/2 cup *Chana Dal*
2 Dried Red Chilli (add more if you want it spicy)
3 pinches of *Hing*
1 ½ tsp Salt (add to taste)
3 tbsp of Oil
½ tsp Turmeric Powder

Method:

○ Soak both the *dals* for an hour.
○ Coarsely grind the *dal* with *hing* (2 pinches) and red chilli without water and set aside.
○ Wash and cut the cluster beans into one centimetre length.
○ Boil for 20 minutes in a pan with turmeric powder and add salt towards the end and let it boil for few more minutes. Drain the water from the beans then set aside.
○ Heat oil in a pan.
○ Add the coarsely ground *dal* and one pinch *hing* for flavour. Roast it till it is golden brown and breaks up/fragments into smaller pieces.
○ Then add the cluster beans and roast it.

Serving Suggestion:

Serve as an accompaniment with *Rasam* rice/ *sambhar* rice/ curd rice. Can also be had with *roti*.

Variation:

To avoid oil, the ground *dal* can be pressure cooked like *idli*.

Did you know?
Health details – Very rich in fibre and is recommended for diabetes. Can be eaten as is like a salad.

PUSHINIKAI KOOTU

  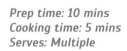

Prep time: 10 mins
Cooking time: 5 mins
Serves: Multiple

Ash Gourd Stew

Ingredients:

3 to 4 cups cubed Ash Gourd, cubed
1 cup *Chana Dal*
1/2 cup Coconut, freshly grated
1 to 2 pieces Green Chilli (add
to taste)
1 tbsp Cumin Seeds
1 tsp Mustard seeds
1 tsp split *Urad Dal*
1 tsp Turmeric powder
1 tsp Salt (add to taste)
5 to 6 Curry Leaves
1 tsp Cooking Oil

Method:

○ Boil the *chana dal* with turmeric powder in a pressure cooker for 7 mins (don't over boil and make it mushy) then set aside.

○ Grind coconut with *jeera* and green chilli into a paste with very little water.

○ Peel and cut ash gourd into cubes and boil it with turmeric powder (discard the inner seeds).

○ Once boiled, add the coconut paste and the boiled *dal* along with salt and let it simmer for few minutes (if *dal* is watery remove the excess water).

○ Let it simmer for a while.

○ To temper, heat the oil in a pan and add mustard seeds, *urad dal*, and curry leaves. Once they splutter, pour over the stew.

Serving Suggestion:

Serve hot with rice. Or as an accompaniment to *rasam* rice.

Variation:

Ash Gourd can be replaced with Bottle gourd (*lauki*) or malabar cucumber.

Did you know?
Health details – Ash Gourd is high in fibre and low in calories. Chana Dal is high in protein and fibre. Both ingredients are good for weight loss and to control sugar. There is just one teaspoon of oil in this dish.
A good summer dish – light and mellow.

VETTAL KHUZHAMBU

Prep time: 5 mins
Cooking time: 20 mins
Serves: 2 people

Ingredients:

250 gms Okra cut into half inch pieces
1 tbsp *Til* Oil
¼ tsp Mustard Seeds
¼ tsp Fenugreek Seeds
A pinch of *Hing*
2 Dry Red Chillies
I tsp *Chana Dal*
A sprig of Curry leaves
Salt to taste
1 tsp *Sambhar* Powder
A lemon sized Tamarind (approx. 32 gms or 1 ½ tbsp)

Method:

○ Soak the tamarind in hot water and squeeze the extract 2 to 3 times adding more water. Throw the remnant fibre. Tamarind extract should be about 2/3 of a cup. Put salt and set it aside.

○ Heat the oil in a pan, add the mustard and fenugreek seeds. Add the red chillies.

○ Once the mustard splutters, add the *chana dal*.

○ When the *dal* turns reddish, add the okra. Stir fry for 5–7 minutes.

○ Add the salted tamarind water and the *sambhar* powder. Give it a stir and let it boil for 7-10 minutes.

○ Garnish with curry leaves.

Serving Suggestion:

Serve hot with rice and roasted *pappadum*.

Variation:

You can put long and thin slices of onion instead of okra.
Do not add *hing* if using onions.

Made by Geetha Krishnan

Tambram's Tip

A spoon of ghee in hot rice adds to the taste of this recipe.

Did you know?
Heath details – this is low in calories.

MOR KHUZHAMBU

Prep time: 10 mins
Cooking time: 20 mins
Serves: 3 people

Buttermilk Curry/South Indian *Kadhi*

Ingredients:

1 cup Ash Gourd/White Pumpkin, cut into half inch squares
3 cups Yogurt
¼ tsp Turmeric Powder
Salt to taste
½ cup Coconut, freshly grated
1 tsp Cumin Seeds
3 Green Chillies

For the tempering:
1 tbsp *Til* Oil
¼ tsp Mustard Seeds
¼ tsp Fenugreek Seeds
A few Curry Leaves
1 dried Red Chilli

Method:

○ In a pressure cooker, put ash gourd and 1 glass of water.
○ Add salt and turmeric powder then boil for 5 to 7 minutes.
○ Whisk the curd into a thick consistency of buttermilk.
○ Grind finely together coconut, green chillies, and cumin seeds then add this to the buttermilk liquid and mix well.
○ Pour this mixture into a deep pan and add the boiled ash gourd pieces and cook on low heat. As soon as it comes to a boil shut the gas. Do not let it boil.

For the tempering:
○ In a small seasoning pan, heat oil and add the mustard seeds and fenugreek seeds. Once they splutter and brown, add the curry leaves and one dried red chilli. Add this to the *mor kozumbu*. Cover it for a few minutes allowing the flavours to infuse.

Serving Suggestion:

Serve hot with rice.

Variation:

○ Can be made with okra, ripe mango, potatoes and drumstick and brinjals.
○ Okra preparation: sauté okra in oil till they are almost cooked. Then add in the curd mixture.
○ For Potato – boil or pressure cook and then peel, chop and add in the *kuzhambu*.

Did you know?
Health details – this dish is made in one teaspoon of oil, which is used for tempering. It is a light and delicious summer curry.

zero OIL DeLIGHT: LaDY T SPeCIALITY

Prep time: 3 mins
Cooking time: 10 mins
Serves: 2-3 people

Potatoes with Skin

Ingredients:

2 large Potatoes
½ tsp Chilli Powder
¼ tsp Turmeric Powder
½ tsp *Hing*
½ tsp Salt (add to taste)

Did you know?
Health details – Cooked potatoes with skin are a source of vitamins and minerals, such as potassium and vitamin C.
Being high in water content, potatoes are primarily composed of carbs and moderate amounts of protein and fibre — but almost no fat.

Method:

○ Take two large potatoes and wash them well.
○ Slice through the centre and cut into small dice pieces along with the skin.
○ Put a pan on the stove. Put potatoes and water just above their level and then add the turmeric, chilli, *hing*, and salt.
○ Cover with the lid and let it boil and cook for ten minutes till it's done. Make sure it does not burn and the water is almost dry.
○ Shut gas. You're done.

Serving Suggestion:

With curd rice, *paruppu sadam*, or *roti*. Or crush a few *thathai* or *murukku*, add the potatoes, put a dollop of thick yogurt on top and have it as a snack.

Variation:

In a *kadai* add oil, mustard seeds and the spices given above. Tip in the potatoes and toss it around for a few mins. Add water- cover and let it cook.

Diced Potatoes

Boiling potatoes

Final Preparation

Beans Poriyal

Prep time: 7 mins
Cooking time: 15 mins
Serves: 2 people

Ingredients:

¼ kg French/Flat Beans
3 tsp Cooking Oil
1 tsp Mustard Seeds
½ tsp *Split Urad Dal*
2 Green Chillies
8 Curry Leaves
¼ tsp Turmeric Powder
½ tsp Red Chilli Powder
Salt to taste
Water
4 tsp Coconut, freshly grated

Tambram's Tip

Don't add too much water to cook beans. It will overcook and get mushy.
For Beans Poriyal to be crunchy, just sprinkle some water, because the beans are already fried in oil for 10 minutes. Coconut should be in garnish quantity only.

Method:

Wash the beans and chop into small round pieces.

Heat cooking oil in a pan on the stove. Add mustard seeds and allow it to splutter.

Now add the *split urad dal* and fry till it is golden in colour.

Put in the chilli and curry leaves & fry for 1 minute, then add the chopped beans and fry for 10 minutes.

Add turmeric powder, red chilli powder and salt. Stir for a couple of minutes.

Add water, just below the level of the beans and allow it to boil for 5 minutes. Wait till the water dries and the beans are well cooked.

Add grated coconut and mix well then switch off the gas.

Serving Suggestion:

Serve hot with rice and *sambhar/rasam/*or curd rice.

Variation:

This dish can be made without coconut if you don't have a preference for it. You can use dried red chillies instead of green. Reduce oil if watching your diet. It cooks well enough in water.

Did you know?
Health details – a good salad option – combination of carbohydrates, protein, and good fats.

cabbage peas poriyal or curry

Simple Cabbage and Peas Stir Fry

Prep time: 10 mins
Cooking time: 15 mins
Serves: 2-3 people

Tambram's Tip

This is a good gluten free and vegan option.

Ingredients:

½ a medium Cabbage
Small cup of fresh or Frozen Peas
½ tsp Turmeric Powder
1 tsp Mustard Seeds
1 tsp *Urad Dal*
2 Green Chillies
3 tbsp Coconut, freshly grated
2 tsp of Cooking Oil
½ tsp of salt (add to taste)

Method:

○ Cut the cabbage into small uniform pieces and soak them in water.
○ If using frozen peas, defrost and keep ready.
○ Take a pan and heat the oil. Add mustard seeds. Once they splutter add *urad dal* and roast till the *dal* is golden brown.
○ Add the cabbage and peas and the salt. Sprinkle water and keep it closed for 5/7 mins just to the point where it is crispy and crunchy.
○ Once cooked, add grated coconut and serve hot as an accompaniment for lunch or dinner.

Variation:

Instead of using peas, soak half a cup of *moong dal* and add it to half-done cabbage and let them cook together.
You can make it into a *kootu* by adding water, grinding the coconut with green chili and adding it after the cabbage has cooked, then allow it to cook for few more minutes.

KATHRIKKAI PODI CURRY

Prep time: 10 mins
Cooking time: 20 mins
Serves: 2 people

Brinjal with Fresh Crunchy Spice Powder

Ingredients:

5 to 6 small Brinjals
3 tsp of Cooking Oil
    Chana Dal
1 tsp of Coriander Seeds
1 tsp of Mustard Seeds
    Urad Dal
2 tsp of Turmeric Powder
1 Red Chilli (add more to spice up)
1 tsp of Salt (add to taste)

Method:

○ Wash the brinjals and dry well. Then cut them into 4 to 6 vertical pieces and soak them in water with turmeric (1 tsp) to prevent oxidisation and discolouring.

○ In a pan add 1 tsp of oil and roast the *chana dal,* coriander seeds, and the chilli till the *dal* becomes golden brown.

○ Take it out and cool it on a plate. Once it cools down, grind coarsely and keep it separately.

○ In the same pan, add the rest of the oil. Add mustard seeds, when it splutters add *urad dal* and let it turn golden brown.

○ Add the brinjals pieces (without the water, salt and turmeric) and sauté it well for 2 mins. Keep cooking it covered in low flame for 3 mins and give it a stir thereafter.

○ Once done, add the ground powder to the brinjal and mix well to allow the powder to wrap around the brinjal. Allow it to be on low heat for 4 to 5 mins.

○ Serve hot with main course.

Variation:

You can make it without the powder and it will become brinjal fry. Very yummy with plain rice or even *roti.*

Did you know?
Health details – Brinjals have a low glycaemic index are high in fibre and low in calories.

Tambram's Tip

You don't need to add coriander seeds, if not readily available– instead add 2 pinches of hing while making the powder. Keeping the dish covered allows a bit of moisture, which helps in cooking and flavour absorption. Be gentle while stirring to ensure that the pieces don't get mashed up as brinjal is fragile. If need be you can add 2 teaspoons of water to allow it to cook. You can make extra powder and store in an air tight container in the fridge for a month.

IDICHaKKa THOran

Tender Jackfruit Stir Fry Kerala Style

Prep time: 30 mins
Cooking time: 30 mins
Serves: 4 people

Ingredients:

1/2 kg Tender Jackfruit (not ripe)
3 Green Chillies (add more to spice up)
1 cup of Coconut, freshly grated
1 tsp Mustard Seeds
1 tsp Cumin Seeds
1/2 tsp Turmeric Powder
1 tsp *Urad Dal*
2 to 3 tbsp of Cooking Oil
1 tsp of salt (add to taste)

Method:

○ First apply oil on your hand before you start preparing the jackfruit. Cut the jackfruit.
Remove the spikey skin as well as hard portion at the centre. Chop them into one square inch pieces along with the seeds, which are tender and delicious.

○ Grind the coconut along with green chillies and cumin seeds. Keep aside.

○ Add turmeric powder and salt and cook the jackfruit with very little water in a pressure cooker.

○ Drain the water, if any left and gently mash it. It should be soft and stringy.

○ In a pan, add the oil. When hot add mustard seeds. When they splutter, add the *urad dal* and sauté it till the *dal* turns light brown.

○ Add the jackfruit and give it a nice stir. After two mins add the coconut paste and mix it well and let it cook for 5 mins with the cover on. Serve hot.

Tambram's Tip

Apply oil to your hand before cutting the jackfruit as it releases a thick sticky milk. It will be easy to cut and the extract will not stick to your hands. Jackfruit tends to discolour, so put the cut pieces in water.

If you need it spicy, can temper it with broken red chillies towards the end. For authentic taste cook in coconut oil.

Did you know?
Health details:
High in protein and fibre
Good option for diabetics
No onion, no garlic dish.
Vegan and gluten free.

PODIMAS WITH POTATO

Prep time: 10 mins
Cooking time: 20 mins
Serves: 3-4 people

South Indian Potato Mash

Ingredients:

4 medium sized Potatoes
2 tbsp of Cooking Oil
1 tsp Mustard Seeds
2 tsp *Urad Dal*
2 tsp *Chana Dal*
½ tsp of Turmeric Powder
2 Green Chillies, broken (Chopped if it is to be spicy)
1 tsp of Ginger, finely grated
6 Curry Leaves
1 tsp Salt (add to taste)

Method:

○ Boil and peel the potatoes, to a point where they are soft.
○ Crush the potatoes to large pieces using a fork. Keep aside.
  Take a pan and heat the oil.
○ Add mustard seeds. When they splutter, add *urad dal*, *chana dal* and fry till golden brown.
○ Add the curry leaves, ginger, chillies turmeric powder and sauté for a minute.
○ Add the crushed potatoes, add salt and give a gentle stir for 2 mins.

Serving Suggestion:

Serve hot with *sambhar* rice or
rasam rice or curd rice

Tambram's Tip

*Be generous with ginger quantity, it
gives the zing required for this dish.*

Variation:

You can add grated coconut if you want.

This dish can be made with sweet potatoes and also raw bananas – you can combine sweet potato and regular potato too.
With the filling you can make the Bombay style toastie sandwich, or stuff it into a *dosa* or *paratha*. Make little fritters or *aloo bonda* by making balls of this mixture, dipping into gram flour batter and deep frying them to a crisp.

Pepper Chicken Drumstick Roast

Chicken Drumsticks Roasted in a Pepper Spice Mix

Prep time: 10 mins
Cooking time: 20 mins
Serves: 4-5 people

Ingredients:

4 Chicken Drumsticks
1 tbsp Peppercorn
2 Green Chillies
3 cloves of Garlic
10 Curry Leaves
Small piece of Ginger
1 tsp of Salt

Method:

- Wash the chicken drumsticks and slit it gently in 2 or 3 places.
- Grind the curry leaves, garlic, ginger, chilli, peppercorn, and salt with little water to make a thick paste.
- Massage the chicken with the paste and ensure it goes into the slits. Marinate the chicken for 30 mins minimum.
- Roast the chicken at 200 degrees F for 30 mins.

Serving Suggestion:

Serve hot with drinks.

Variation:

Instead of curry leaves use fresh coriander leaves.

Tambram's Tip

Keep a bit of the marinade paste and coat the drumsticks mid-way through the roasting process for better absorption of the flavour.
If you don't have an oven or grill, use a grilling pan on the stove.

Did you know?
Health details – zero oil process.

BULLSEYE

Amma's Quick Breakfast

Prep time: 10 mins
Cooking time: 10 mins
Serves: 1 person

Ingredients:

2 Eggs
2 tsp *Ghee*/Oil
Salt to taste
Pepper to taste
Chili Flakes

Did you know?
Health details – Good source of protein.

Method:

○ Take a deep non-stick spoon, like the one you use for tempering.
○ Turn on the gas on low flame and add one spoon of *ghee*/oil.
○ Break the egg and pour it inside the spoon, while centring the yolk. It should take 2 to 3 mins to cook and become solid.
○ Sprinkle salt/pepper/chili flakes on top.
○ Take a blunt knife and circle around the egg disengaging it from the sides of the spoon. Then flip it and cook on low flame for a minute.
○ Remove it gently onto a plate.

Heating Spoon

Sprinkle salt/pepper/chili flakes on top

Eggs

Deep Non-Stick Spoon

Mutta Curry

South Indian Egg Curry

Prep time: 10 mins
Cooking time: 10 mins
Serves: 1 people

Ingredients:

3 to 4 tbsp Cooking Oil
½ tsp Fennel Seeds (optional)
½ tsp Mustard Seeds
1 Onion, chopped fine
1/2 Tomato, chopped fine
½ inch Ginger, chopped fine
1 pod of Garlic, chopped fine
8 Curry Leaves
½ tsp Turmeric Powder
8 to 10 Black Peppercorns, lightly crushed
1 Green Chilli
1 tsp Red Chilli Powder (optional)
2 Eggs, full boiled
½ tsp Salt
2 sprigs Fresh Coriander Leaves

Method:

○ In a pan heat the oil.
○ Add the mustard and fennel seeds and let them splutter.
○ Add pepper corn, green chili, and turmeric powder.
○ Sauté the onion till it is golden brown.
○ Add tomato, ginger, garlic, curry leaves, and salt. Cook until the tomatoes become soft.
○ Add half a cup of water and bring it to a boil for 3 mins.
○ Add the boiled eggs and cover it for 3 or 4 mins. Add little water if it becomes dry.

Serving Suggestion:

Serve hot with rice or *appam* garnished with fresh coriander leaves.

Variation:

You can lightly fry the eggs before immersing them in the curry for cooking. If you like coconut milk you can add a quarter cup to this recipe – after the tomatoes have softened.

Tambram's Tip

Make two cuts on the eggs for the ingredients to seep in. Make sure not to cut it through.
To make hard boiled eggs – place the eggs in a saucepan large enough for them to have space. Add water to cover them by an inch. On high heat let it come to a boil. Wait for a minute and switch off gas. Cover pan. Let the eggs stand in hot water for about 10 mins.

Did you know?
Health details – Rich source of protein, antioxidants, and amino acids.

pepper CHICKeN in COCONUT milk

Prep time: 10 mins
Cooking time: 20 mins
Serves: 2 people

Ingredients:

250 gms of Chicken or 4 Drumsticks
2 cups of thick Coconut Milk
1 tbsp of Peppercorn
1 Green Chilli (or more to taste)
3 Cloves of Garlic
12 Curry Leaves
Small piece of Ginger
1 tsp of Salt
2 regular size Onions
2 or 3 tbsp of *Ghee* or Cooking Oil

Method:

○ Grind the garlic, curry leaves, ginger, pepper and chilli into a paste adding very little water, if required.
○ Wash the chicken well.
○ Peel and cut the onion into long thin slices, heat the cooker and add ghee or cooking oil and sauté the onion till gold brown.
○ Add the paste and the chicken and salt and sauté it for 5 to 7 mins.
○ Add three fourths of the coconut milk, then close the lid and cook for 6 or 7 whistles. Once it cools down, open and check for salt. Add more, if required.
○ Add the rest of the coconut milk and let it simmer for a minute or two.
○ Add 3 or 4 curry leaves and a few peppercorns for visual appeal.

Serving Suggestion:

Serve with steaming hot white rice/*dosa/appam*.

Variation:

Can be made with lamb instead of chicken.

Tambram's Tip

I prefer cooking this dish in Ghee, which in right quantities is considered to be a health food.
Do not use coconut milk in cans which is meant for Thai cooking. If you have access to only this form of coconut milk, add more chillies to cut the sweet taste or it will make the dish sweet.

Did you know?
Health details– White meat is lean meat.
And after years of bashing, coconut is considered a healthy ingredient.

EDITOR'S CHOICE: KOSHA MANGSHO AND DOSA

Bengali Style Slow Cooked, Melt-in-the-Mouth Mutton Curry

Prep time: 10 mins
Cooking time: 20 mins
Serves: 4-5 people

Ingredients:

1 Kg Mutton
4 medium Onions
3 Bay leaves
5 Cloves
1 tsp Sugar
4 medium Potatoes, halved
1 tsp Garam Masala
4 Green Cardamom
½ inch Cinnamon Stick
1 cup Mustard Oil

For the marination:

10 Cloves Garlic
2-inch Ginger
2 tsp Turmeric Powder
2 tsp Coriander Powder
2 tsp Red Chili Powder
2 tsp of Salt (add more to taste)
1 cup of Yogurt (dahi)
2 tbsp of Mustard Oil
1 tsp of Sugar

The dosa is a near-perfect dish. If you make it crispy with ghee it gets even more delicious. But I discovered the way it tastes best. Why eat *Mangsho Jhol* or *Kosha Mangsho* only with plain rice or roti? Why not combine it with a dosa? In one fell swoop, you get *dal* too.

Anyway, let me not rationalize this. Believe me, it's a gastronomical delight! The Tambram Dosa and the Bengali Mutton curry. A wonderful confluence of both our cuisines. Go ahead. Have a mouth party. In case you are vegetarian and have the stomach for the gravy only, give it a try too. *Write in and let me know what you thought!*

Method:

○ Grind ginger & garlic together in a mixer to a smooth paste.

○ Cut the mutton to the right size; wash and clean the mutton.

○ Add all the ingredients listed under marination to the mutton and leave it for at for atleast 2 to 3 hours till it all gets absorbed.

○ Heat 2 tbsp mustard oil in a cooker/ pan. Fry the potatoes till they turn golden brown. Keep them aside.

○ Add the remaining mustard oil in the cooker and add thinly sliced onion and pan fry them till it turns golden brown. Add all the condiments like clove, cardamom, a bit of turmeric, chili powder, bay leaf and temper them. Add sugar to give the gravy the nice brown colour to it. Add the potatoes and give it a stir.

- Add the marinated mutton. And keep stirring it over low flame for a prolonged time till the meat turns white and fully integrates with the onion/condiment. (The word *Kosha* means stir frying over time) This will take 20 / 25 mins of constant stirring it.
- Add water to fully submerge the mutton and close the cooker and let it cook for at least 20 mins / 9 to 10 whistles approx. Post that check if meat is cooked or else cook for more time Add freshly chopped coriander leaves.

Serving Suggestion:

Serve with crisp or soft *dosas*.

A wonderful confluence of both Bengali and Tambram Cuisines.

Tasty accompaniments to
Tambram cuisine

Rice with rasam or curd or sambhar - and a little crunch on the side. Lemon rice, tamarind rice, coconut rice, or tomato rice with pickle and crunchiest accompaniments really add to the taste or completeness of the meal.

Or better still, just have them by themselves as an in-between snack......

Appalams and Papadams

The *Appalams* of Tamil Nadu are made of *urad dal*. Apart from salt, they do not have any added spices. They can be fried, roasted, or microwaved. At 6 inches diameter they are thin and crunchy. Sandy in colour with a smooth finish, they give a very delicate mouthfeel.

Kerala's *Papadams* , made from *urad dal* with no spices, are different in that they are a little thicker, smaller in diameter (approx. 5 inches), and not as smooth as *appalams*. These can be fried, roasted, or microwaved too.

When they cook in hot oil, they "puff up" or curl when they are done. They have a thicker crunch and are yellowish in colour.

My daughter busts an entire *appalam* into tiny pieces and spreads it over her sambhar rice and makes a meal of it.

Variety of raw papadams in the market

Karavadams

The Tambram's method of frying them:

The Tambram has an amazing way to fry them so that they don't crunch up and curl. To watch him make these is like an *appalam* or *papadam* frying ceremony! To begin, large, cavernous, air tight, steel boxes are lined up in the kitchen to store them. A big *kadai* which has smoking hot oil is made ready; kitchen towels are lined up on the granite slab next to the stove. He cuts each raw *appalam* into two halves. Then, using a pair of steel tongs he immerses one half in the hot oil, and very quickly, as it cooks, he turns it to the other side. Within a few seconds, he lifts it out of the hot oil and places it on the paper towel for the excess oil to drain off. Once it cools, it makes its way into the boxes. While it may not take much time from start to finish, the skill and drama that goes into making the perfect *appalam* or *papadam* is worth a watch, especially in the hands of The Tambram!!

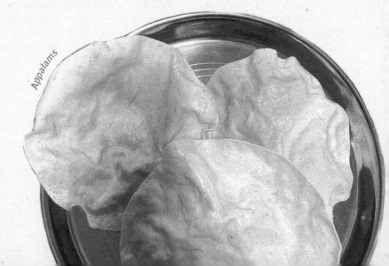

Appalams

Mor Milagai

Mor Milagai is a delicious crisp chilli which is marinated in yogurt and sun-dried. For 5-8 days. They are also available ready-made in packets. These sun dried chillies are fried in oil and are a wonderful complement to curd rice.

It is one of the most popular condiments of the South Indian Cuisine.

Mor Milagai

Manathangalikkai

Sundakkai

Vathals

According to Geetha Krishnan, my sister-in-law, "The lady's finger and aubergine were quite common at my home, along with the rest.
I use *sundakkai* and *manathangalikai* ever so often in *vathakuzhumbu*. Also fry them to have with curd rice or *parappu sadam* (*dal* rice)".

Vendakai (lady's finger)

The table alongside was made by her as a reference to all the accompaniments used with meals.

A lot of our Non-South Indian friends and relatives like to eat these just by themselves and not during meal times. They are happy to have them as "Tiffin items" along with tea or coffee.

VATHAL		COMMON NAME
Sundakkai	:	Turkey Berry
Manathangalikkai	:	Nightshade
Pavakkai	:	Bitter gourd
Kothavarangai	:	Cluster beans
Thamarai kizhangu	:	Lotus stem
Vendakai	:	Lady's finger/ Okra
Kathirikkai	:	Aubergine/ Brinjal
Tayir/ Mor Millagai	:	Chilli

Store bought snacks as side dishes to rice preparations like Banana chips and potato chips are a great crunch additive.

Potato Chips

Banana Chips

Process takes time. The right time to flip the dosa will determine if it's undercooked or tasty.

Enjoy each step. It makes all the difference!

TIFFIN/ snack

SOUTH INDIAN TIFFIN
WHAT IS THIS UNIQUE CONCEPT?

When I got married and entered the Tambram world, I came upon so many new concepts. For example, there was always talk around "What will we have for tiffin?" Now, to me, tiffin had always been that box that I carried to school with something to eat during break time. So, it baffled me and intrigued me why a meal at home was named tiffin?

Tiffin, I figured, was a throwback from the British era. Derived from the word "Tiffing", which meant a small drink, it also was a slang term for sipping in the 18th century. In colonial India, it took on a meaning of a light luncheon to start with, due to the difference of weather between England and India. Because of the heat, light meals were considered appropriate in the daytime. Soon it evolved to representing a light tea-time meal at about 3 pm, or to a light breakfast consisting of typical tea-time food items.

Actually, I call it transition food. A between meals treat that usually consists of all the delicious goodies!

Idlis, Dal Vadas, Aloo Bondas, Pakodas, Bhajji, Thaiyar Vadas, Dal Vadais, Keerai Vadais, Upma, String Hoppers, a dry sweet, *Sundal*, Mixtures, *Karvadams, Murukku, Nada Pakodas, Thattai Omapodi*, and so many more options! In the old days, every one of these items would be made at home. Now, with so much commercial production, all the typical fast foods are tiffin foods.
Light snacks. Light meals. Still the best when made by your own prowess. So, go ahead and learn or try some of the easy tiffin recipes from our kitchen. And enjoy the delicacies made by your own hands!

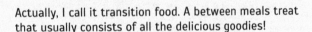

Medu Vada

Sign Boards

Mini Tiffin Meal

Tiffin boxes, usually multi-layered, are packed with dry snacks and taken for picnics. In the days gone by, long-distance travel by train was a ceremony in itself. Planning the tiffin items to be carried on the train would take a lot of discussions. Sometimes one travelled two nights to reach the destination.

The Tambram's Grandfather would have rice put into the tiffin containers with milk and a bit of setting curd. Thus, on the second day, he would open it and fresh curd rice would be ready in the tiffin carrier, which would be accompanied by mango *avakkai* pickle or lemon pickle!

Whenever I travel in South India, little eateries have signboards placed outside saying, "Meals and Tiffin-Ready". Some very popular food chains are called Tiffin Houses. And the sought-after ones are packed with customers!

Now people are becoming experts in tiffin services whereby delectable items can be ordered online. But in our Tambram household, the term tiffin is that in-between meal with one or two goodies which you eat with great relish, in the early evening. And it has to be accompanied with a cup of steaming hot south Indian filter coffee in a steel tumbler and dawara.

Rava Idlis

Aloo Bonda

Thate Idli

Masala Dosa Aloo

Prep time: 15 mins
Cooking time: 5 mins
Serves: 2–3 people

Accompaniment Stuffed into Dosa

Ingredients:

3 medium Potatoes, boiled
1 medium Onion, sliced lengthwise
2 Green Chillies
8–10 Curry Leaves
½ tsp Mustard Seeds
¼ tsp Turmeric Powder
1 tsp *Urad Dal*

1 tsp *Chana Dal*
1 inch Ginger, cut into tiny pieces
2 tbsp fresh Coriander Leaves, chopped fine (optional)
Juice of one Lemon (optional)
1 tbsp Oil
Salt to taste

Tambram's Tip

Add the stuffing into a crispy dosa just before eating or else it will make the whole dosa soggy. You can also serve the masala separately.

Method:

○ Crumble the potatoes slightly. They should be partly mashed and partly large pieces.

○ Heat oil in a pan. Add mustard seeds, and let them splutter. Add *urad dal, chana dal* and toss it till the *dals* become light brown. Then add green chillies, curry leaves and fry it for a minute.

○ Now add onions, turmeric powder, and salt and fry it for 3 minutes or till onions turn soft.

○ Add two cups of water and when it starts boiling add the mashed potato and mix well with the other ingredients. Cook for 4 to 5 mins then put off the gas.

○ Add coriander leaves, squeeze lemon juice and mix well.

Variation:

You can add tomato pieces instead of lime juice.

IDLI Upma

Prep time: 5 mins
Cooking time: 10 mins
Serves: 2 people

Typically the old *idlis* are made into *Idli Upma*
(crumbling idlis consumes more oil but is also tastier)

Ingredients:

4 to 5 *idlis* (a day or so old),
cut into small squares

3 to 4 tsp cooking Oil

½ tsp Mustard Seeds

1 tbsp *Urad Dal*

1 Dried Red Chilli

2 pinches *Hing*

15 Curry Leaves

Salt to taste

Did you know?
Health details – idlis are good for gut health as they are made from fermented dough.

A little history– My mother always freshened older idlis at home with this quick tiffin idea!

Method:

○ Heat oil in a pan. Add mustard seeds and wait until they splutter, then add *urad dal*. Roast in low flame until slightly brown.

○ Add red chili broken into pieces, *hing* and curry leaves. Then add the *idli* pieces and salt.

○ Sauté till it becomes slightly crisp

Serving Suggestion:

Serve with hot filter coffee.
You can sprinkle chutney powder (*molagapodi*) on top to give it a spicy flavour.

Variation:

Instead of dicing the *idlis* into cubes, you can crumble them unevenly with your fingers and prepare it in a softer version.

Tambram's Tip

Don't cover while cooking, as it will become soggy.
A quick snack to rustle up when you have unexpected guests!!

WHITE CHICKPEA SUNDAL

Prep time: 10 mins
Cooking time: 5 mins
Serves: Multiple

Ingredients:

1 cup of Chickpeas
1 Dried Red Chilli
2 tsp *Urad Dal*
1 tsp Mustard Seeds
Pinch of *Hing*
1 tsp Salt
2 tsp of Cooking Oil
6 to 8 Curry Leaves
1 Green Chilli (optional)
1/8 cup Coconut, grated (optional)

Method:

○ Soak the chickpeas overnight or at least for 5 to 6 hours.
○ Boil it in a pressure cooker for 10 mins, then set aside.
○ Heat oil in a pan and add mustard seeds. Once they splutter, add *urad dal, hing*, small pieces of red chillies, and curry leaves. Adding green chilli is optional.
○ Once the *dal* is golden brown add the boiled chickpeas and salt and sauté it for a few minutes.
○ Garnish with coconut and serve hot.

Serving Suggestion:

Serve in bowls with freshly brewed filter coffee.

Variation:

Can be made with *kala chana*.

Did you know?
Health details – The nutrition value is high; it contains fibre, protein, carbohydrates, and minerals. it is good to control cholesterol.

UPMA KOZHAKATTAI

Prep time: 5 mins
Cooking time: 10 mins
Serves: 2 people

Ingredients:

1 cup measure of *Idli–Dosa* Rice
(to make about 20)
½ cup Coconut, freshly grated
4 to 5 tsp Cooking Oil
½ tsp Mustard Seeds
1 tbsp Broken Cashew Nuts
1 Dried Red Chilli
2 Green Chillies
2 pinches *Hing*
15 Curry Leaves
Salt to taste

Method:

○ Soak the *idli-dosa* rice overnight.
○ Drain the water and spread it out on a cloth to drain out most of the moisture, however, don't make it bone dry.
○ Make a coarse grainy powder in a wet grinder.
○ Heat oil in a pan. Add mustard seeds and wait until they splutter. Add curry leaves, *hing* and put the broken cashew and roast until slightly brown then add red chilli broken into pieces. Add green chilli, depending on how spicy you want it.
○ Add the ground flour and a little water.
○ Add coconut and cook on medium flame for 10 minutes, then add salt.
○ Cool for 8 to 10 minutes and make them into fist balls.
○ Then steam it in an idli cooker for about 10 minutes.

Serving Suggestion:

Serve with hot filter coffee.
You can sprinkle chutney powder
(*molagapodi*) on top to give it a spicy flavour.

Tambram's Tip

Don't wait for the mixture to become cold, then you can't make them in a fist ball.

A quick snack to rustle up when you have unexpected guests!!

Did you know?
Health details – idlis are good for gut health as they are made from fermented dough.

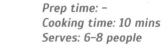

Tambram Family Mixture

Prep time: –
Cooking time: 10 mins
Serves: 6–8 people

A Tasty Savoury Snack

Ingredients:

6 cups of Puffed Rice
I cup *Omapodi/Bhujia*
1 cup Peanuts
¼ tsp of *Hing*
8 Curry Leaves
2 Dried Red Chillies or 1 tsp Chilli Powder
A pinch of Salt
1.5 tbsp of Oil

Method:

○ Heat oil in a big pan. Add the *hing* powder, chilli powder, and the curry leaves.
○ Add in the puffed rice and roast it for 6–8 minutes, stirring and tossing continuously.
○ Heat 1/2 tsp oil in a smaller pan and fry the peanuts. Remove from heat and let everything cool down.
○ Add salt to the puffed rice.
○ Now tip in the peanuts and add the *omapodi/bhujia*.
○ Mix well and store in an airtight box when it cools down fully.

Variation:

You can add roasted *chana*, raisins, and small pieces of fried coconut or green chillies. You can also put dry roasted cashew nuts.

Did you know?
Health details – Good mix of carbs and protein with hardly any oil. If you are on a diet, just dry roast and make the entire dish without oil.

Tambram's Tip

To make it filling, you can add small pieces of cucumber, onion, and tiny, diced boiled potatoes. You can also garnish it with tomato (put it on top and don't mix as it will make the mixture soggy). Put these just before serving. Don't store the mixture with these additives.
Don't put too much of these into the mixture or the crunch will reduce! This makes a good meal in itself. Inspired idea from Bengali "Jhaal Mudi"!

panirayam

Prep time: 10 mins
Cooking time: 10 mins
Serves: 3

Rice and Lentil Dumplings

Ingredients:

1 ½ cups thick *Idli/Dosa* batter
I Green Chilli, finely chopped
2 sprigs Coriander Leaves, chopped
1 small Carrot, finely grated
1 medium Onion, finely cut

3 Curry Leaves, torn into tiny pieces
A pinch of Salt
A pinch of *Hing*
½ tsp Mustard Seeds
1 tbsp Oil for frying

Method:

○ Heat oil in a pan. Add mustard seeds and pieces of curry leaves. Once the mustard seeds splutter, add the onions and carrots and sauté till it's cooked without browning. Add *hing* and salt.

○ Turn off the gas then add the coriander leaves.

○ Mix in the sautéed vegetables. The batter should be is thick, not runny.

○ In a *paniyaram* pan, put a drop of oil in each cavity and coat it well. With a tablespoon drop a dollop of the dough into each cavity filling it three fourths. Make sure you leave enough space for the dough to rise.

○ Turn on flame to medium, partly cover the pan with a lid, and let it cook for 2 mins. You will notice holes forming in the dough. Take a spoon or kitchen tongs and gently flip the dumplings. Let it cook for another 3 mins.

○ Switch off gas when the balls are golden. This ensures they are crispy outside and soft inside.

Tambram's Tip

*Use leftover batter to make this dish. A quick prep when unexpected guests come over. Use any veggies at home. Even shredded spinach.
Serve with filter coffee.*

Serving Suggestion:

Serve it hot with chutney, or *molagapodi*. Or just by itself.

Did you know?
Health details – very little oil in each dumpling. Mainly prepared by steaming. This filling snacks is good for gut health due to fermentation.

Variation:

The same recipe can be made with *rava/sooji/semolina* – If you take a cup of *rava*, take three-fourth cups of yogurt and mix well. Let the batter sit for 20 mins.
Add the veggies and follow the same process as above. Sweet paniyaram can also be made by adding thickened jaggery, fresh grated coconut and cardamom powder to the batter.

IDIYAPPAM

Rice Sevai or Rice Noodles

Prep time: 5 mins
Cooking time: 5 mins
Serves: 2 people

Ingredients:

100 gms of instant Rice *Sevai*
1/2 cup of Coconut, freshly grated
1 Green Chilli broken into 2 pieces
1 Red Chilli broken into 2 pieces
12 Cashew Nuts
1 tbsp *Chana Dal*

1 tsp *Urad Dal*
½ tsp Mustard Seeds
Pinch of *Hing*
2 tsp of Oil
8 Curry Leaves
½ tsp Salt (add to taste)

Tambram's Tip

I crush the red chilli into smaller pieces while roasting and crush the green chilli to let out the flavour. I like to use instant sevai.

Method:

○ Boil water in a pan. Add ½ tsp of oil and the instant *sevai*. Typically, it will take 4 to 5 minutes for the *sevai* to cook without becoming mushy.

○ Remove from heat and drain the water using a sieve or fine colander. To ensure the *sevai* stays separate and does not stick together, spread on a plate. Let it cool down.

○ Heat the remaining oil in a pan and put in the mustard seeds. Once they sputter, add the cashew nuts and then both the *dals*. Roast till they are becomes brownish red.

○ Add *hing* and curry leaves and switch off the stove.

○ Now add the cooked *sevai* and salt and then gently mix it.

○ Add the coconut and toss the mixture on low heat for a minute or two, then serve.

PURE RICE SEVAI

Serving Suggestion:

Serve it hot. In this recipe, I have suggested rice *sevai* as a tiffin item. Rice *Sevai* is also served as a meal along with coconut milk and jaggery or with strong tamarind gravy.

Variation:

You can make it with lemon and serve it as lemon rice *sevai*. Add ½ tsp of turmeric while roasting and one teaspoon of squeezed lemon juice at the end and serve.

We can add peanuts instead of cashew nuts.

ADAI

Prep time:-
Soaking: 4 hrs
Grinding/ fermenting: 1.5 hrs
Cooking time: 3 - 4 mins/Adai

Ingredients:

2 cups *Idli Rice*
1/2 cup *Split Urad Dal*
1/2 cup *Tuar Dal*
1/2 cup *Chana Dal*
3 to 4 Dried Red Chillies
3 pinches of *Hing*
Salt to taste
A sprig of Curry Leaves (optional)

Variation:

You can make it only with rice, without any *dal*. Add *methi* (fenugreek) seeds and use the same process.

Serving Suggestion:

Serve hot with white butter or honey.

Method:

To prepare the batter:

○ Soak rice for 3 to 4 hours. Soak all the *dals* together in another container for the same period of time.

○ Grind the rice coarsely with a little water along with red chilli. Grind the *dals* even more coarsely along with curry leaves.

○ Mix both the batters along with salt and *hing*. Set it aside for an hour and let it ferment a bit. The batter has to be thick, unlike dosa batter.

To prepare the *adais*:

○ Heat a flat pan and spread the batter into a large circle.

○ Put oil around the *adai* and let it cook for a minute or two till it turns golden brown.

○ Flip over to the other side and let it cook for a minute more.
Take off the pan once golden and cooked and serve hot.

Tambram's Tip

I usually soak tuar dal and chana dal for 2 hours and grind it with hing and red chillies and mix it with leftover idli batter. Add salt to taste and prepare adai.

My mother used to make holes after spreading the batter, whereas I cover it with a domed lid.
This way it cooks well uniformly.

Did you know?
Health details – A great option as a filling snack or a meal. It has a good mix of carbs and proteins.

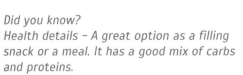

MINI MEDUVADA

Bite-Sized Savoury Snack

Soaking: 5 hrs
Prep time:: 15 mins
Cooking time: 25 mins
Serves: 6-7 people

Ingredients:

1 cup *Urad Dal*
½ tsp of Salt (add to taste)
Oil for deep frying
½ tsp of Peppercorn, lightly crushed

Serving Suggestion:

Serve it hot with coconut chutney for breakfast or for tiffin.

Variation:

For some extra flavour and texture you can add finely chopped onions, after finishing the grinding.
This is called onion vada and it takes a bit longer to cook.

Method:

○ Soak the *urad dal* for 5 hours.
○ Then wash it well and grind it into a smooth paste, without much water. You can add 2 or 3 teaspoons of water. Add salt while grinding itself. Towards the end add pepper and the dough is ready for frying.
○ Take a deep pan and pour oil in a good quantity. Once the oil heats up, add a bit of dough to see if it rises, which means it is the right temperature.
○ Rub a small quantity of unheated oil on your palm to moisten it, then take a small amount of the dough, pat it into a small disc and gently slide it into the oil. Be careful not to burn yourself!
○ Making a round hole in the centre of the disc will allow it to cook well. (I don't, instead, I make smaller discs and call it *mini meduvada*).
○ Fry by turning them around till they are golden brown and crispy. Depending on the size of the pan, each batch can make four to five *vadas*.
○ With this quantity, you will get 15 to 18 mini *vadas*.

Tambram's Tip

Amma used to place a bit of dough in water. What I call The Float Test. If it floats well, means it is of the right consistency, and you're ready to go ahead.

The oil test- too hot will burn the vada; too cold and the vada will not cook well. So the trick is to watch it as it heats up, and not get to a burning point.

DaL VaDa

Prep time: 15 mins
Cooking time: 25 mins
Serves: 6-7 people

Crunchy Cocktail Lentil Snack

Ingredients:

1/2 cup *Chana Dal*
1 Red Chili
A Pinch of *Hing*
5 Curry Leaves (optional)
1/2 teaspoon Salt (add to taste)
Oil for deep frying

Method:

○ Wash and grind the *dal* coarsely with green chili, *hing* and salt. Then mix in the curry leaves.
○ Heat the oil in the pan and keep it on medium flame.
○ Take a small amount of dough in your palm and press it into a small disc.
○ Slip it into the hot oil and fry it on medium flame in batches of 4 to 5 *vadas*.
○ Turn the sides and fry till they are golden brown and crisp. With this quantity, you can make 15 to 20 cocktail *vadas*.

Tambram's Tip

I grind half of the dal into a smoother paste and the other half into a coarse paste.
This allows better binding and the vadas don't disintegrate.
Take it out in a paper towel to absorb extra oil.

Serving Suggestion:

Serve it as a snack with coffee/tea or even a drink in the evening.

Variation:

You can add onion and ginger and green chili and call it *masala vada*.

Wake Up
TO SOUTH INDIAN
FILTER COFFEE

Coming from a tea-drinking home, I transitioned to a Coffee or *Kaapi* drinking one after I got married. Having a hot cup of coffee, when I woke up, in a steel tumbler was alien to my usual experience of drinking tea in a ceramic mug! The piping hot coffee was served in a small steel glass with a steel bowl placed below it almost like a saucer. I soon learned the glass was called a tumbler, a term not so common in my spoken English and the steel bowl below was a *dawara*. In my husband's home, they referred to steel as eversilver – I had never heard this term before. I got used to this delicious beverage and actually started loving it. The process of making it is as engrossing as the taste. I learned how to make this type of coffee and want to share it with you.

The coffee powder has such aroma that once the box is opened the kitchen is enveloped in its fragrance. In my in-laws' house, a good quality powder was procured from a local store that roasts the beans and grinds them coarsely. Some customers prefer a blend that has a bit of chicory added to the coffee powder. This adds a woody, nutty taste and is actually good for health. Chicory also gives a darker colour to the coffee!

Ingredients:

3 tablespoons coarse medium ground (powder)
1 cup water
Half cup milk
1 tsp sugar or to taste

Prep time: 45 mins
Cooking time: mins
Serves: 2 people

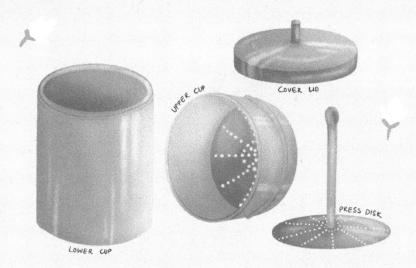

LOWER CUP

UPPER CUP

COVER LID

PRESS DISK

To start with, you need the South Indian Filter Coffee Maker. It's a simple steel utensil and is available at any vessel store or even online. There are two parts to this gadget. The top section has tiny holes at the bottom through which the coffee filters down. There is a small umbrella-like object inside which is used to press the coffee down. The decoction gets collected in the lower section.

Method to Prepare the Best Filter Coffee
Wash and wipe clean the utensil. Then take two tablespoons of coffee powder for one cup of coffee. So if you are making two or three cups, I suggest you put in at least 5 heaped tablespoons of coffee powder in the upper half of the container. Use the tiny umbrella-like object to press the coffee powder down. Then fix the upper section on top of the lower one. Now, take boiling hot water and pour it in the upper section; fill it to the top. Shut the lid and wait for at least 45 minutes. A clear and rich coffee decoction will collect in the bottom layer. If you want your cup of coffee immediately on waking and can't wait for the aromatic decoction liquid to form drop-by-drop, set up the filtration process at night! Some people prefer this.

Now take the steel tumbler and pour in hot milk and a little bit of hot water. Add the decoction to your taste. Mix 5 tbsp coffee decoction with half cup milk, adjusting as per the strength of coffee desired. I prefer to put almost equal parts of the brew to the milk. Add sugar to taste.

Now comes the fun part of getting a frothy top! The act of mixing the coffee by pouring it and pulling the delicious liquid from one tumbler to the *dawara* three to four times. This distance is supposed to represent a meter. Locals also call this meter coffee!!

This action actually blends all the ingredients well, cools the coffee, and creates a thick froth. Please note if you overdo it the coffee can get cold.

At times you can take a second decoction from the coffee in the filter by pouring more hot water, though this decoction will be lighter!

FOOD IS FUEL.
WHATEVER YOU
CHOOSE TO EAT,
HAVE IT WITH JOY
AND GRATITUDE.
AND NEVER FEEL
GUILTY.

PICKLES/ CHUTNEYS

INSTANT MANGO PICKLE

Prep time: 10 mins
Cooking time: 5 mins
Serves: 6 people

Ingredients:

2 medium size Raw Mangoes
Salt to taste
½ tsp *Hing*
5 tbsp *Til* Oil
1 tsp Chilli Powder
¼ tsp Turmeric Powder
1 tsp Fenugreek Seeds
1 tsp Mustard Seeds

Method:

○ Wash and dry the mangoes. Peel the skin (can make it with skin too). Slice mango into thin ½ cm strips/cubes. Set aside.
○ In a pan, heat *til* oil. Then put in the mustard seeds and let them splutter.
○ Add turmeric powder and chilli powder. Then add *hing* and *methi* seeds to the oil. Now add the mango pieces.
○ Put the salt and sauté it for 3 mins on low heat.

INSTANT NELLIKAI URUGAI

Prep time: 10 mins
Cooking time: 25 mins
Serves: 6 people

Serving Suggestion:

Serve with curd rice.

Ingredients:

4 to 6 *Amla* cut as vectors or like orange segments
6 to 8 tsp *Til* Oil
¼ tsp Fenugreek Seeds
½ tsp *Hing*
2 to 3 tsp Red Chilli powder
½ tsp salt

Method:

○ Heat a deep pan. Add oil. When oil is hot, add fenugreek seeds and wait for them to splutter.
○ Add *hing* and chilli powder.
○ Add *amla* segments and salt.
○ Sauté till *amla* is cooked.

MANGAI THOKKU

Grated Raw Mango Pickle

Prep time: 10 mins
Cooking time: 15 mins
Serves: 6 people

Ingredients:

1 large Raw Mango (I use *kili mookku/ Totapuri* mango)
3 tbsp of Cooking Oil (I prefer to use *Til* oil)
¼ tsp *Hing*
¼ tsp *Methi* Powder
1/2 tsp Turmeric Powder
2 tbsp of Salt (add to taste)
1 tsp of Mustard Seeds
3 tbsp of Red Chilli Powder

Method:

○ Wash and dry the mango. Then peel and grate it and keep aside.
○ In a pan, put one spoon of oil. Add mustard seeds and *Hing*. When the mustard seeds splutter, add the grated mango.
○ Now add turmeric powder, chili powder, and salt and stir it well on a low flame.
○ Let the mango cook. After a few minutes add the remaining oil, then allow it to cook until it is a nice fibrous paste. Add methi powder and switch off the stove.

Serving Suggestion:

Serve as accompaniment to curd rice/lemon rice.

Tambram's Tip

Generally, the KIli mooku/Totapuri mango is a bit sweet and not very sour. If any other mango is being used, I add a tablespoon of sugar. Though adding sugar reduces the shelf life. Adding til oil generously helps preserve this pickle in the fridge for a long period.

paruppu Togayal

Lentil and Coconut Chutney

Prep time: 5 mins
Cooking time: 15 mins
Serves: 3–4 people

Ingredients:

1 cup *Tuar Dal*
¼ to ½ cup Coconut, freshly grated
2 to 3 Red Chillies
2 tsp Cooking Oil
4 to 5 Peppercorn (optional)
2 pinches of *Hing*
Salt as required

For the tempering:

½ tsp *Urad Dal*
2 tsp Oil
1 tsp Mustard Seeds
2 Dried Red Chilli

Method:

○ Add oil in a pan and fry the chillies and *dal* till it becomes brownish.

Take it off the stove and let it cool on a plate. Once cooled, grind the *dal*, chilli, and *hing* along with salt. After one grind add coconut and grind again coarsely with a little water.

For the tempering:

○ In a small pan heat oil. Add mustard seeds, *urad dal* and dried red chilli. Let the mustard seeds splutter.

○ Then pour the tempering over the chutney and serve with *idli and dosa*, *vada*, and *pongal*.

Serving Suggestion:

Serve as accompaniment or with hot rice and *ghee*.

COCONUT CHUTNEY

  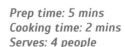

Prep time: 5 mins
Cooking time: 2 mins
Serves: 4 people

Ingredients:

1 cup Coconut, freshly grated
3 Green Chillies
½ tsp Salt
¼–½ cup Water

For the tempering:
2 tsp Oil
1 tsp Mustard Seeds
2 Dried Red Chilli
few Curry Leaves
½ tsp *Urad Dal*
½ tsp *Chana Dal*

Method:

○ In a grinder, blend to a smooth paste coconut pieces, green chillies, salt, and water, Add more water as required.

For the tempering:
○ In a small pan heat oil. Add mustard seeds, *urad dal, chana dal*, dried red chilli, and few curry leaves. Let the mustard seeds splutter.
○ Then pour the tempering over the coconut chutney and serve with *idli and dosa, vada*, and *pongal*.

Tambram's Tip

Try and use fresh coconut as it's juicier and healthier. Add the tempering just before serving so that it doesn't lose its crunch.

Variation:

You can add:
○ A few roasted peanuts on top, for additional crunch.
○ Also, you can add a small ball of tamarind and grind it with the coconut for a tangy flavour.
○ You can also add garlic and onion cut into tiny pieces and grind it in with the coconut.

Did you know?
Health details – Coconut is considered a source of healthy fat. It contains protein and fibre, as well as minerals such as iron, manganese, copper and magnesium.

FOOD IS
SWEET
MEMORIES

sweets

Rava Ladoo

Prep time: *10 mins*
Cooking time: *25 mins*
Serves: *Multiple*

Ingredients:

1 cup *Rava*
½ cup *Ghee*
1 cup Sugar
2 pinches Cardamom Powder
2 tbsp Cashew Nut broken into small pieces (optional)

Method:

○ Dry roast the *rava* in a pan on low heat till it turns slightly golden in colour.
○ Ensure that you keep stirring and quickly take it off the stove when it is done.
○ Allow it to cool down.
○ Add the sugar. Now grind the *rava* and the sugar into a coarse powder.
○ In a pan, roast the cashew nuts golden brown and set aside.
○ Add the *ghee* and cashew nuts to the *rava*-sugar mixture and make them into small balls pressing them into shape in your palm. Be quick while forming the mixture into balls. It is best to do so in 2 batches.
○ Store in dry container.

Did you know?
Health details – essentially carbohydrate and sugar. Bit of fat and protein.
This gives instant energy and can be eaten on the go.

pori urundai

Crunchy balls made from puffed rice

Prep time: 10 mins
Cooking time: 25 mins
Serves: Multiple

Ingredients:

4 cups Puffed Rice
1 cup Jaggery
¼ tsp Cardamom Powder (optional)
¼ tsp Dried Ginger Powder (optional)

Did you know?
Health details – this is a zero oil snack.

Method:

○ Place the puffed rice in a wide mouthed bowl. Set aside.

○ Pour half a cup of water into a pan. Mix in the jaggery, cardamom powder and dried ginger powder, then boil it.

○ The mixture will starts to get thicker as it cooks. Keep stirring. Put a few drops of this mixture in a small cup or plate of water. If it solidifies, it is done. (My mother used to try and roll it with her fingers to reach the stage where it solidifies into a tight firm ball).

○ Put off the flame and pour the mixture into the bowl of puffed rice and mix it well immediately.

○ Mix well with a spoon carefully as the syrup is very hot. While the mixture is still hot, take a handful and make them into balls. Apply enough pressure to form round balls without crushing.

○ Depending on the size of the balls you can get 10 to 16 *pori urundais.*

Variation:

Quarter cup finely chopped coconut, lightly fried, can be added.

Tambram's Tip

Apply ghee or rice powder on your palms before forming the balls. This will ensure that the rice puff and jaggery mixture does not stick to your palms.

Roll into ladoos while the mixture is hot. If it gets cold, it will crumble and you won't be able to shape them.

sweet sundal

Sweet Black Eyed Peas

Prep time: 3 mins
Cooking time: 20 mins
Serves: 2 people

Ingredients:

1 cup Black Eyed Peas
3/4th cup of Jaggery
1 tsp *Ghee* (optional)
1 tsp of Cardamom Powder (optional)

Method:

○ Boil the peas for 10 to 12 mins in water.
○ Dissolve the jaggery in half cup of water and boil it, till it thickens for about 5 to 7 minutes.
○ Add cardamom powder.
○ Drain the water out from the peas and add the jaggery. Mix and stir it well for 3 to 4 minutes.
○ Put in the *ghee* before turning off the gas.

Serving Suggestion:

Serve as a snack/dessert in a small bowl.

Tambram's Tip

Stir the jaggery and keep looking at consistency. If it becomes too thick, add a bit of water.

Did you know?
Health details – Jaggery increases the metabolic rate. Black eyed peas contain antioxidants like flavonoids, which help the body fight diseases. Low in calories.

PaL Payasam

Prep time: 5 mins
Cooking time: 25 mins
Serves: Multiple

Sweet Milk Kheer

Ingredients:

1/4 cup Rice
6 cups of Milk
10 Cashew Nuts
2 tbsp of Raisins
1 tbsp of *Ghee*
¼ tsp of Cardamom Powder (optional)
½ cup Sugar (Add more to taste)

Method:

○ Wash and soak the rice in water for 15 mins.

○ In a pan, roast the cashew nuts till they are golden brown.

○ Towards the end add the raisins. Raisins will swell. Set aside.

○ Pour the milk in a pan and boil it.
Keep stirring and let it not overflow.

○ Allow it to boil on an open flame and condense a bit and then add the soaked rice without the water.

○ Allow the rice to cook in the milk. it will take 12 mins or so.

○ Once rice is cooked add the sugar and stir it for 3 or 4 mins, till sugar dissolves completely.

○ Add the roasted cashew nuts, raisins and cardamom powder and give it a stir.

○ Serve hot or cold.

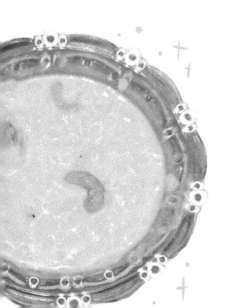

Variation:

If you like saffron, add a few strains soaked in milk at the end when the dish is ready.

You can substitute rice with semolina. Then it is called rava payasam.

Tambram's Tip

You can make it with condensed milk too. In which case cook the rice in water and drain the water.

kesari

Prep time: 10 mins
Cooking time: 10 mins
Serves: 3-4 people

Traditional Sweet made of Semolina

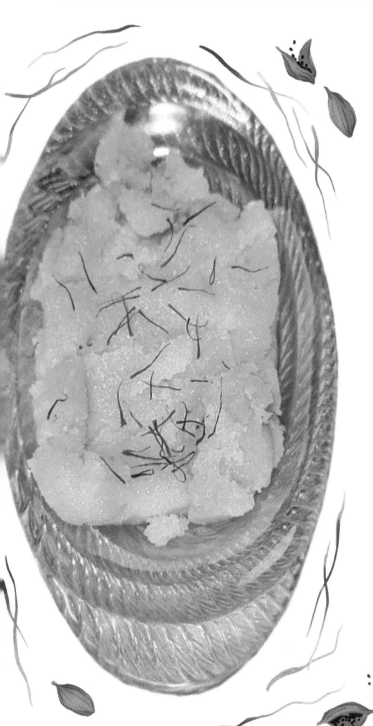

Ingredients:

1 cup Sugar
1 ½ cup Water
4 Cardamoms, powdered in the mortar pestle
1 ¼ cup *Ghee*
Half cup *Rava/Sooji*
15 Cashew Nuts
Saffron Strains or pinch of Colouring Agent

Method:

○ Soak saffron strains in 2 teaspoons of water till it starts turning yellow.
○ In a pan, first roast the cashew nuts in a bit of *ghee* to golden brown and keep aside.
○ In the same pan pour the remaining *ghee* and roast the *rava* till it changes colour a bit.
○ In another pan boil the water with sugar. Once it boils add it to the pan with *rava*, slowly to ensure no lumps are formed.
○ Add roasted cashew nuts and cardamom powder and keep stirring. Then add the saffron strains or the colouring agent and let it all cook till the *rava* is cooked and looks fluffy.
○ Garnish with some saffron strains for presentation.

Serving Suggestion:

Serve it warm as dessert.

sweet Aval

Prep time: 10 mins
Cooking time: 25 mins
Serves: Multiple

Quick and Delicious Flattened Rice Sweet

Ingredients:

1 cup of *Aval*
½ cup of Coconut, freshly grated
¼ cup of Jaggery (add more to taste)
¼ tsp of Cardamom Powder

Method:

○ Wash the *aval* and spread it thin on a towel and let it dry.
○ After it dries but is still moist add grated coconut, jaggery, and cardamom powder.
○ Pound it gently in an *imam dasta* (mortar pestle) till it all integrates.

Serving Suggestion:

Serve it as a snack or dessert.

Tambram's Tip

Coconut has to be fresh.

It is served during Gokulashtami/ Krishna Jayanthi as Lord Krishna was very fond of it.

Did you know?
Health details – Zero oil cooking.

My grandfather was very fond of sweets and wanted to eat a treat every day, albeit in small quantities. Because of his long tenure of living in the North, my grandmother created some fun concoctions of the region – almost instant sweets – but very, very tasty.

INSTANT MALPUA

Prep time: 5 mins
Cooking time: 5 mins
Serves: 1 person

This was made whenever we fried *puris*

Ingredients:

2 *Puris*
A Cup of Milk (after condensing)
3 tbps of Sugar
10 Raisins (optional)

Method:

○ In a bowl, add the sugar to the milk while it is still warm and stir it well till sugar dissolves.
○ Add the puris and let it soak well in the milk then add the raisins and serve warm or cold.

Tambram's Tip

Can be made with condensed milk.

INSTANT SHAHI TUKDA

Prep time: *5 mins*
Cooking time: *7 mins*
Serves: *1 person*

Ingredients:

Half Cup of Milk (after condensing)
A small layer of Cream/*Malai*
1 slice of Bread
2 tbps of Sugar (add more to make it sweeter)
8 Raisins (optional)
1/2 tsp of crushed *Pista* or Roasted Almonds (optional)

Method:

○ Toast the bread slice in a toaster till it becomes golden brown and crisp.

○ In a bowl add the sugar to the milk, while it is still warm, and stir it well till sugar dissolves.

○ In a flat plate place the toast and pour the milk on top, along with the cream/*malai*.

○ Add the raisins and sprinkle the crushed *Pista*/Almonds and serve it cold.

Tambram's Tip

Can be made with condensed milk.

Let the toast cool down to retain the crispiness.

THE DELECTABLE MEDLEY OF
SOUTH SNACKS

Hand Nazhi

Murukku

Omapodi

Jackfruit chips

My mother-in-law used to regale me with stories of how she would make all these at home. She made Murukku and banana chips during her growing years in Manjeri, Kerala. But the rest of the snacks were whipped out with the use of the hand Nazhi contraption with ease.

My sister-in-law, Sushma Rajagopalan, who used to assist her mom in these culinary delights told me, "As a child this was one of my favourite play things. I would fill it with all kinds of dough - atta, rice flours, etc., and make shapes."

I got introduced to the delicious flavours and taste of snacks from Tamil Nadu and Kerala post my marriage. Evening tiffin time would always be a hot cup of filter coffee with a bubbling frothy layer on top and some snacks on small steel plates, such as, Madras Mixture and *Omapodi*, which is the equivalent of *Bhujia* but has crunchy curry leaves and a tinge of hing.

Varieties of *Murukku* in different shapes – round or long; sometimes in multiple layers and even small sized ones! *Thatai, Sheedai*, and Banana chips that were either yellow or white. Long Plantain chips or Jackfruit chips salted or sweetened with Jaggery. Tapioca chips and so many more!!

Somehow, I feel that apart from *murukku* and banana chips, which are well-known and consumed all over India, the others varieties of snacks have not got their due in terms of popularity. Every Indian buys and consumes *bhujia, khatta meetha mix, chakli, mathi*, etc., but has perhaps missed out on some of these Southern options.

I call them the hidden secrets of Indian treats.
Perhaps one needs to take a trip to a South Indian store or restaurant to pick them up. Online options are available now. And if you are planning to buy, try a good South Indian brand.

So dear readers, take note. There is an amazing world of crunchies out there. Try them, be adventurous, and make them. But don't miss out on these hidden Indian treats!!

Seedai

Madras Mixture

Tapioca chips

Sakrattuperi

Glossary

#No.	English	Hindi	Tamil
1	Asafoetida	Hing	Perungayam
2	Clarified butter	Ghee	Nei
3	Coconut	Nariyal	Thengai
4	Coconut milk	Naariyal ka doodh	Thengapāl
5	Cumin seeds	Jeera	Jeeragam
6	Curry leaves	Karipatta	Karivēppilai
7	Fennel Seeds	Sauf	Peruñcīrakam
8	Fenugreek seed	Methi	Vendhayam
9	Garlic	Lehsun	Poondu
10	Ginger	Adrakh	Inji
11	Green chilli	Hari mirch	Pachai milagāi
12	Gunpowder	Idli powder	Molagapodi
13	Jaggery	Gurh	Vellam
14	Mustard seeds	Rai	Kadugu
15	Onion	Piyaaz	Vengāyam
16	Peppercorn	Kali Mirch	Milagu
17	Puffed rice	Murmure	Pori
18	Rasam powder	Rasam masala	Rasam Podi
19	Red Chilli	Lal Mirch	Kanja Shivappu Melagai
20	Red Gram Lentil	Tuar Dal	Thuvaram paruppu
21	Split Bengal Gram Lentil	Chana Dal	Kadalai Parrupu
22	Split Black Gram Lentil	Urad Dal	Ulutham Parrupu
23	Chickpeas Lentil	Chole	Sundal
24	Sambhar powder	Sambhar masala	Sambhar Podi
25	Sesame Seed	Til	Ellu
26	Tamarind	Imli	Puli
27	Turmeric	Haldi	Manjal
29	Yogurt	Dahi	Tayir
30	Salt	Namak	Uppu

1	Idli stand	5	Flat spoons
2	Dosa Tava	6	Mixer/ grinder/ blender
3	Paniyaram Pan	7	Coffee Filter
4	Scoop spoon	8	Steamer

9	Deep pan/wok/kadai
10	Tadka Pan

List of Ingredients used in Tambram Recipes

#No.	English	Hindi	Tamil
1	Ash Gourd	Safed Kaddu	Pushinikai
2	Bay Leaves	Tej Patta	bē ilakaꞏ
3	Beetroot	Chukandar	Beetroot
4	Black Eyed Peas	Lobia/Raungi	Karamani
5	Bottle Gourd	Lauki	Sorakaya
6	Brinjals/Aubergine/Eggplant	Baigan	Kathirikkai
7	Buttermilk	Chaash	Mor
8	Cardamom powder	Elaichi powder	Elakkay Podi
9	Cashew nut	Kaju	Mundiri Parruppu
10	Coriander Leaves	Dhania Patti	Kothamalli
11	Cluster beans	Gavar Phalli	Kothavarangai
12	Cloves	Laung	Kirāmpu
13	Cinnamon Stick	Dal Chinni	Ilavankappattai kucci
15	Dried ginger powder	Sonth	Sukku Podi
16	Drumstick	Saragwa or Sehjan	Murungakkai
17	French Beans	phansi	Beans
18	Flat Beans	Sem	Avarakai
19	Fenugreek powder	Methi powder	Vendhaya Podi
20	Flattened rice	Poha	Aval
21	Green Gram Dal	Moong Dal	Paasi paruppu
22	Honey	Madhu	Ten
23	Indian Gooseberry	Amla	Nellikkai
24	Kerala Banana	Kerala ka kela	Nendhra Pazham
25	peanuts	Moongphalee	Verkadalai
26	Potato	Aloo	Urulai Kizhangu
27	Red Pumpkin	Kaddu	Parangikkai
28	Radish	Mooli	Mullangi
29	Raw Banana	Kaccha Kela	Vazhaikkai
30	Rice Noodles	sevai	sevai
31	Semolina	Rava	Rava
32	Spinach	Palak Saag	Keerai
33	Taro Roots	Arbi	Chepung Kazhangungu
34	Vermicelli	semiya	semiya
35	Jackfruit	Kathal	idichakka
36	Eggs	Anda	Muttai
37	Chicken drumsticks	Murgi ke taang	Kozhi Kaal
	Mutton	Gosht	Attu Iracci

ACKNOWLEDGEMENTS

Firstly, I would like to thank all our friends and relatives who have loved eating this kind of cuisine at our place. Who have asked for the same dishes they like on repeat mode. You gave us the confidence to bring out this book.

But I'm getting ahead of myself. Mita my sister, the credit at first goes to you for saying let's get all of Sundar's recipes together. For reaching out for recipes especially *aloo* rice and tomato *pachadi* for Moina. To my brother Probir, who has so much excitement to come to Delhi and eat "Sundi food" even when he turned vegan. Love you both.
To my father-in-law and mother-in-law. Who had their own areas of culinary expertise and these have made their way into this book too. To their love for me for mastering *idlis* and *dosas*. Which I learnt from them. For the basic recipes that I hand wrote and still have from them – which are also featured in this book. We often talk about their yummy *sambhar*. Best in the world!

To Sundar's family – Ajit and Geetha, Sushma and Vijay, Anoop and Karishma thanks for your wonderful reactions to the idea and cover designs when I presented them over a family call. Especially to Geetha for helping me understand the *Vettals* better and the photo of your tasty *Vettal kozhambu* featured in that recipe. Equally to Sushma for helping me with the snack making at their home as children and all the implements used in making them.

Now to how the book actually got done. Having written "Dolly's table" a memories book on my mother with a section on her signature recipes, I was overwhelmed with the amount of feedback I got from people. They sent in photos of what they had tried and the excitement of the taste they savoured. It brought so much joy all around. I learnt a lot from that experience and thought why not give this idea its proper place in the sun. I spoke about my thoughts with The Tambram - being sure he would nix it. But to my greatest surprise he was excited willing and ready. To go beyond a Word document.
I was clear this book had to be beautifully presented. I wrote out a five-page creative brief for myself. Once I was clear on my idea, of this book being positioned for the youth firstly and then for everyone who would like to know and cook this type of food I shared it with The Tambram and Lady T.
They agreed with my concept.

I knew while I was writing it and Sundar was cooking the dishes, we would need a fresh young perspective for the cover design, and overall art direction. I didn't have to look too far. I zeroed in Kartika Bagodi. A highly talented young girl with a commercial art degree to boot. She is my cousin Jayati Mukherjee's daughter. I spoke with young Uma aka Kartika and asked if she like to join my team in this effort. She jumped in. I can't describe what she has brought to this job. Enthusiasm, and a brilliant work ethic. But most of all oodles of talent. All the illustrations you see in the book are hers. Don't those tomatoes and onions look real? She took all the suggestions and feedback with an open mind. We met every 5 days on lengthy calls to work and progress the book. Recipes and ingredients and food shots going from here and layouts getting generated there. We live in different cities. And slowly and steadily the weeks rolled on – but she kept her eye on the ball. My cousin Pinky aka Jayati, joined in on the progress meetings each time and

was enjoying the creativity and discussions. Out of sheer helpfulness she started collating the recipes and pictures, and when it got too chaotic, she set up the entire project management on this book. Google drives and excel sheets for all the material. Messages coming from her with "you still need to send pictures for xyz recipe"- "We need standard phrases – do we say mustard seeds crackle or splutter or sputter? - wait let me do a little research" She tried a number of our recipes as we sent them. *Olan*, Coconut rice, *Adai, Sambhar*, and a few more and gave us a double thumbs up each time. Being a master's in fine arts her creative inputs on the cover design and other aspects were beneficial.

Having decided this book is for young and busy people primarily - and of course for everyone else – I was researching the name, cover designs (we did 20 options) ease of recipe grasping - with a panel of youngsters between 23 and 39. A big shout out to Lady T's friend's circle who were so quick with their feedback. All the youngsters in the family too. You guys are the best. To my family who saw the PDF files on screen share mode – from across the globe to many "oooooooo's" and "ahhhhhh's" to messages saying, "When is this book coming out?" To helping me get a perspective on many issues. Moina and Amol thanks for responding so quickly with the edits on the opening piece. Arup, EB, Moina Amol, Debjani Armaan, Sushmita -and the babies-of the family, all my love. You are my A team. Aditi thanks for the enthusiasm and asking for and trying some of the recipes in this book.

To the Tambram and Lady T. You know how much I had to learn for this book. From food photography, to recipe formats to the articles I have written which required research to the appropriate plating for each dish- it's been a new learning. (This book is fully produced by us at home – and my niece and cousin). For both your words of encouragement and pushing me along. For Raya, hours of watching your antics continents away on video calls has been my stress buster and happy zone.

To my parents. There would be no me without you. For everything I know and everything I do, is because of you. Always in my heart.

ABOUT THE AUTHOR

Jayshree Mukherjee Sundar is the Tambram's wife. She is a Bengali who has had fun integrating into Tamil culture and cuisine.

She is an MBA from Jamnalal Bajaj Institute of Management Studies and had a long and successful career in Advertising in firms like Lintas and Leo Burnett. Thereafter she transitioned to academic life and is a visiting faculty at top business schools.

In the last two years she has written three books – the first one "Dolly's Table" met with resounding success. The other two are in the pipeline to be published soon.
While in Advertising she had a number of published articles in leading papers and websites. She also has lively social media posts. Her hashtags #indiaisbeautiful❣ #jmscomments #movieswithjms are very popular.

She calls herself a keen observer of life.

Watching and learning from her husband's culinary skills has been a treat. So she decided to share the experience and bring this art to you.